Upper Crusts

A CAPITAL LIFESTYLES BOOK

Upper Crusts

Fabulous Ways to Use Bread

Delectable Recipes for Appetizers, Soups,

Salads, Main Courses, Desserts, and More

SHEILAH KAUFMAN

CAPITAL BOOKS, INC.

STERLING, VIRGINIA

Capital Books, Inc.
P.O. Box 605
Herndon, Virginia 20172-0605

ISBN 10: 1-933102-39-X (alk. paper)
ISBN 13: 978-1-933102-39-9

Library of Congress Cataloging-in-Publication Data

Kaufman, Sheilah.
  Upper crusts : fabulous ways to use bread : delectable recipes for appetizers, soups, salads, main courses, and more / Sheilah Kaufman.
      p. cm.
  ISBN-13: 978-1-933102-39-9 (alk. paper)
  ISBN-10: 1-933102-39-X (alk. paper)
  1. Cookery (Bread) 2. Bread. I. Title.

  TX769.K3255 2007
  641.8'15—dc22

                                                    2006038632

Printed in the United States of America on acid-free paper that meets the American National Standards Institute Z39-48 Standard.

First Edition

10 9 8 7 6 5 4 3 2 1

To my family—

Barry, Debra, Jeffrey, T.J., and Kaleb

BREAD AND PROMISES

Flour, water and salt
Meet yeast,
Then dough stirs alive
In your hands
Rises to your needs
Breathes with mystery and
Emanates sweet grapey scent
Like a stranger, waiting in your kitchen.

Dr. Gail Bellamy,
EDITOR OF *Restaurant Hospitality*

CONTENTS

Foreword

Nothing brings people together like a good meal or a fabulous buffet table at a holiday party, and no one knows this better than Sheilah Kaufman.

Many years ago, in Texas, Sheilah and I bonded over a shared love of food and have kept in touch ever since. We share recipes, read each other's work, and often find ourselves teaching at the same schools.

I always look forward to Sheilah's latest cookbook, and I'm particularly pleased to introduce you to *Upper Crusts: Fabulous Ways to Use Bread—Delectable Recipes for Appetizers, Soups, Salads, Main Courses, Desserts, and More.* As far as I know, there isn't another book like it. This wonderful new book takes our universal passion for bread and applies it to simple yet elegant recipes that will enhance any occasion. Sheilah uses the "staff of life" in the most ingenious and delectable ways. She has found ways to use both fresh and leftover bread to liven up any everyday meal or special occasion.

This is NOT a bread-baking book. Staying true to her "fearless and fussless" tradition, Sheilah works with many types of store-bought bread for almost every recipe. She also brings her famous international versatility to this collection of recipes by including Greek, Turkish, Sephardic,

Mexican, Mediterranean, and English specialties (be sure to try the Scrooge-inspired Christmas pudding!). I especially enjoyed the historic tidbits about the cultural importance of bread, woven throughout the book, and the many handy cooking tips.

Sheilah invited many of her longtime friends in the cooking world to contribute their favorite bread-based recipes. Featured in the pages of *Upper Crusts* are recipes from Patrick O'Connell, of the Inn at Little Washington, in Virginia; Henry Haller, retired White House chef; and Michel Richard of Citronelle in Washington, D.C., to name just a few.

Looking through the pages of *Upper Crusts* was like sharing a visit with my good friend, whose warmth and wisdom I'm glad to share with you.

Enjoy,
Sally Bernstein
Editor in Chief, Sally's Place
Sallys-Place.com

ACKNOWLEDGMENTS

*S*incere thanks to Sandra Greeley for the title and her support, and to Naomi Weiss, Naomi Tropp, and Karen Braun for their wonderful editing.

To Paula Jacobson, Sharon, and Amy for testing recipes, and Eileen and Barry Barry for eating them.

To the wonderful chefs, authors, and friends who gave me recipes.

To Debra Friedman of Sturbridge Village, Sturbridge, Massachusetts, and Kathleen Curtin of Plimoth Plantation for so much help with the history.

And to Kathleen Hughes, who made it all happen!

INTRODUCTION

> *"Bread is the staff of life; in which is contained, in-*
> *clusive, the quintessence of beef, mutton, veal, veni-*
> *son, partridge, plum-pudding and custard."*
>
> —JONATHAN SWIFT

*U*pper Crusts is a joyous, user-friendly collection of recipes using bread in all its versatile guises—from the familiar to the chic, inventive, and seductive; from hometown favorites to exotic international surprises. The recipes can grace any meal or festive occasion and can be prepared with virtually fool-proof success by novices as well as gourmet cooks, professional chefs, bed-and-breakfast proprietors, gourmet markets, or restaurateurs looking for new ways to enhance the foods they serve.

The History of Bread

Bread, in one form or another, has been a principal source of food for man from earliest times. This book celebrates its long history and the inventiveness of cooks through the ages.

In the Stone Age, people made solid "cakes" from stone-crushed barley and wheat. A millstone used for grinding corn has been found that is thought to be 7,500 years old. Historians feel that the ability to sow and reap cereals may be one of the chief reasons for man to dwell in communities, rather than to live a wandering life hunting and herding cattle. This "food" could be stored and used through the winter months and made in abundance in the summer ones. Did civilization begin here?

Wheat has been found in pits where human settlements flourished 8,000 years ago. Bread, both leavened and unleavened, is mentioned numerous times in the Bible. Loaves and rolls have been found in ancient Egyptian tombs. And, in the Egyptian galleries of the British Museum, one can view actual ancient grains of wheat as well as loaves of bread that were made and baked over 5,000 years ago. Much of the knowledge we have about Egyptian bread and bread baking comes from the philosopher Athenaeus, who lived in the third century CE. He wrote that the best bakers were from Phoenicia or Lydia, and the best bread-makers from Cappadocia. He gives us a list of the sorts of bread common in his time: leavened and unleavened loaves, loaves made from the best wheat flour, and loaves made from groats, rye, or even from acorns and millet. We learn of lovely crusty loaves too, and loaves baked on a hearth. It is no surprise that the trade of the baker is one of the oldest crafts in the world.

In Old Testament times, evidence points to the fact that bread-making—preparing the grain, making the bread, and baking it—was the work of women; but in the palaces of kings and princes and in large households, the bakers' duties would be specialized. Bread was leavened; that is, an agent in the form of a "barm" was added to the dough, which caused the mixture to rise in the shape of our familiar loaf.

Buried ruins like Pompeii have revealed the variety of bakeries existing in those times, including public bakeries where the poorer people brought their bread to be baked, or from which they could buy ready-baked bread.

The Romans enjoyed several kinds of bread. The wealthy and privileged liked rich breads made with milk, eggs, and butter, and always favored white bread made from wheat. In ancient Greece, a keen rivalry existed between cities as to which produced the best bread.

The ancient Greeks and Romans used bread as a staple and argued over the virtues of white bread vs. brown bread. Apparently, the appeal for white bread is not a modern fad: the Greeks and Romans both liked their bread white. Color was one of the main tests for quality at the time of Pliny (CE 70), who wrote: "The wheat of Cyprus is swarthy and produces a dark bread, for which reason it is generally mixed with the white wheat of Alexandria." Plato (c. 400 BCE) pictured the ideal state where men lived to a healthy old age on wholemeal bread ground from a local wheat. Socrates, however, suggested that this proposal meant the whole population would be living on pig food.

A Bakers' Guild was formed in Rome about 168 BCE. From that point on, the industry existed as a separate profession. As freemen, the bakers in Rome, during this period, enjoyed special privileges, but once a baker joined the Guild or College neither they nor their children could leave the profession and/or take up other trades. As privileged as they were, members of the Guild were forbidden to mix with "comedians and gladiators" and were prohibited from attending performances at the amphitheater, where they could be "contaminated by the vices of the ordinary people."

Much later, during the reign of King John of England (1202), laws were passed regulating the price of bread. Recurring periods of famine due to natural causes were frequent at this time, and the ruling classes knew that rebellion often followed famine. They hoped to keep the lower classes quiet by keeping the price of bread from rising too high. Stringent regulations were passed concerning the weight of bread. Fines were levied for improprieties. Men could be placed in the pillory with slabs of dough around their necks, while women were sent to Newgate prison.

Later, with the development of the steam engine and the growing of large quantities of wheat on the prairies of America, white flour (and bread) could be produced at a price that put it in the hands of everyone—not just the rich. And today wheat is grown all over the world, with different varieties growing in different climates.

This rich, long history has produced an equally rich diversity of recipes. I have enjoyed reviewing recipes dating back hundreds of years, showing that stale bread has long been a staple in man's diet, appearing as a thickener in soups, as "fried bread" (croutons) to make soups more substantial, as stuffing, as bread pudding, and as a meal unto itself as a bowl of bread and milk (in the same way we serve cereal today). The recipes I have chosen for this book (some old, some new) are just a few of the wonderful uses for bread in today's ever-evolving cuisine. I hope you enjoy them as much as I enjoyed testing and tasting them all.

While this book was written as a kosher book, several of the people who supplied me with their wonderful recipes (from their books or collections) asked that they be left in their original form, which I have, with appropriate notes for changes. If you are not kosher, butter may be used instead of margarine, and cream or half-and-half instead of a non-dairy cream substitute.

Sheilah Kaufman

Bread Crumbs

"The ambition of every good cook must be to make something very good with the fewest possible ingredients."

—Urbain Dubois

*B*read crumbs have many uses in cooking. They are a quick, nutritious thickener for soup or sauces, casseroles, and meatloaves. They are used for breading, frying, topping, or coating other ingredients. In addition, bread crumbs are used in a number of steamed and baked puddings. In many steamed desserts, bread crumbs are used in place of some or all of the flour. Some recipes call for the crumbs to be dry—others call for the crumbs to be fresh and soft.

How to Prepare Bread Crumbs

I never purchase unflavored bread crumbs, but prefer to make my own. They are quick and easy to prepare—as well as being an economical use of stale or extra bread. I always keep a bag in my freezer in case I decide to prepare one of these fabulous dishes on the spur of the moment. Seasonings can be mixed in according to the recipe you are making.

To prepare fresh bread crumbs, simply break fresh bread into pieces and run them through a food processor.

To prepare dry bread crumbs, preheat the oven to 225°F, then dry slices of bread until firm and crisp to the touch. Let the bread cool, break into small pieces, and process in the food processor or blender until finely crushed; or crush into crumbs with a rolling pin.

1 slice dried bread = about 1/3 cup dried bread crumbs

1 untrimmed slice of fresh bread = about 1/2 cup fresh bread crumbs

Bread crumbs can be refrigerated (tightly sealed) for a week, or frozen for six months or more. I prefer saving them either of those ways. But, if you prefer leaving your bread crumbs out, remember to save them in a paper bag, never a sealed container. This allows the air to circulate through them and protects from (or delays) mold.

Almond Celery Stuffing

My friend Paula Jacobson is a cooking teacher, food editor, and recipe tester, who loves to cook, bake, and entertain. She was a great help in "giving birth" to this book. Paula's cousin, Susan, got this recipe from *The Gourmet Cookbook*, which was published in 1950. The original recipe was for a chicken, squab, or guinea hen; and it was to be doubled for a goose or turkey. Paula always doubled the recipe for a twelve-pound bird, and quadrupled it for a twenty-pound bird. Since she no longer stuffs the turkey, she makes six or seven times the recipe and bakes it in a large greased casserole or roasting pan.

2 & 1/2 cups bread crumbs*
2 tablespoons margarine, melted
3/4 cup almonds, blanched, toasted, and fincly chopped
3/4 cup (approximately 3 big bunches) ground celery tops (leaves)
3 tablespoons dry white wine or vermouth
1/3 teaspoon poultry seasoning
1 large egg
1 teaspoon salt
1/3 teaspoon crushed peppercorns
2 tablespoons finely chopped onion
1 clove garlic, mashed or pressed

*To make bread crumbs: Using home-style white bread, cut thick slices and then cut into squares. Place in a blender or processor and pulse until you have coarse crumbs. Toss crumbs with the margarine.

To make the stuffing: Combine all ingredients, mixing well. Stuff in neck and cavity of turkey.

Apple Brown Betty

No one remembers who Betty was, but a Brown Betty is both layered and topped with sweet buttered crumbs. In this recipe (and others), it is important for the crumbs to be dry since they will absorb the juices from the middle and bottom layers and remain crunchy on top.

1 & 1/2 cups dry unseasoned bread crumbs
6 tablespoons unsalted butter, melted
1 & 1/4 cups dark brown sugar, packed (sift if lumpy)
1 teaspoon ground cinnamon
1/2 teaspoon ground nutmeg
1/4 teaspoon ground cloves
1 pound apples (about 3 medium apples), peeled, cored, and sliced
3 tablespoons fresh lemon juice, divided in half

Place your oven rack in the lower third of the oven and preheat the oven to 350°F.

In a medium size bowl, mix the bread crumbs and butter.

In a small bowl, whisk together the sugar, cinnamon, nutmeg, and cloves.

Spread one third of the crumb mixture evenly over the bottom of an 8x8-inch baking pan or a 9-inch pie pan.

Place half of the apples over the crumb mixture and sprinkle with half of the sugar mixture.

Drizzle on 1 & 1/2 tablespoons of lemon juice and cover with another third of the crumb mixture, the rest of the apples, and the rest of the sugar mixture.

Drizzle on the remaining lemon juice and cover with the remaining crumb mixture.

Cover the pan with aluminum foil and bake until the apples are nearly tender, about 40 minutes.

Uncover the dish, increase the oven temperature to 400°F and continue baking until the Betty is browned, about 15 minutes. Great served with vanilla ice cream.

Serves 6.

 To keep brown sugar from hardening, store it in a container with a tight-fitting lid, along with a piece of bread.

Artichoke Nibblers

These are as popular now as they were when I began making them over forty years ago. I make these ahead and freeze them so I can pull them out for unexpected guests.

2 jars (6 ounces each) marinated artichoke hearts
1 small onion, finely chopped
2 garlic cloves, finely chopped
4 large eggs
1/4 cup unseasoned dry bread crumbs
salt
freshly ground pepper
1/4 teaspoon dried oregano
dash of Tabasco or other hot sauce to taste
2 cups grated sharp cheddar cheese
2 tablespoons finely chopped parsley

Preheat oven to 325°F. Grease a 9x9x2-inch baking pan.
Drain the marinade from one of the jars of artichokes and place the liquid in a skillet.
Drain the other jar, discarding the liquid. Finely chop the artichoke hearts and set aside.
Heat the artichoke liquid and sauté the onions and garlic, stirring, for 3 minutes.
Remove from the heat.
In a large bowl, beat the eggs well, add the bread crumbs, salt, pepper, oregano, and Tabasco sauce, mixing well. Stir in the cheese, parsley, artichokes, and the onion mixture.
Pour mixture into prepared pan.
Bake for 30 minutes, remove from oven, cut into squares, and serve immediately.
Squares can be refrigerated for future use and served cold or reheated for 10 to 12 minutes at 325°F. Nibblers can be made ahead, baked, cooled, and then frozen if desired.
Makes about 36.

Dried spices are stronger than fresh spices, so use only 1/4 the recommended amount of dried when substituting for fresh spices.

Cabbage Strudel

This easy strudel can be made ahead and frozen. Shelly Sackett, owner of Kitchen Affairs, in Evansville, Indiana, shared this recipe with me when I was teaching a phyllo class. It makes a great appetizer that everyone likes, including those who dislike cabbage.

2 pounds cabbage, shredded
2 teaspoons salt
2 tablespoons canola oil
1/2 cup sliced scallions
freshly ground pepper
8 sheets phyllo, defrosted, at room temperature
2 cups fresh bread crumbs (approximately)
melted butter

Preheat oven to 350°F. Toss the cabbage with salt and let stand 15 minutes. Squeeze out as much moisture as possible.

Heat the oil in a large skillet over medium heat, add cabbage, scallions, and pepper, and sauté 5 to 6 minutes.

Lay phyllo sheets out, long side toward you. Butter one sheet, top with sprinkling of bread crumbs, lay a second sheet over the first, butter, top with crumbs, repeat until you have used 4 sheets.

Spoon half the cabbage mixture down on the long side about 4 inches from one side. Roll up strudel and place seam side down on a greased baking sheet.

Brush top with melted butter and sprinkle with bread crumbs. Repeat with remaining sheets and filling to make a second strudel.

Bake in preheated oven for 45 minutes or until golden brown. Allow to stand 10 minutes. Cut into 1 & 1/2-inch to 2-inch slices on an angle and serve hot.

Serves 6 to 8.

Cauliflower Patties

My friend Vivi gave me the recipe for these creamy patties. They have a nice outer crust and a light interior. When made with matzah meal, this is a typical Sephardic recipe served for Passover called *Fritada di Cauliflor*.

1 large cauliflower, broken up
3 large eggs, beaten
1 cup dry bread crumbs or matzah meal
salt
freshly ground pepper
canola oil for frying

NOTE: You might want to use more salt and pepper than you normally would in a recipe.

In a large pot, cook the cauliflower until soft in salted boiling water, about 15 minutes.
Drain well and mash in a food processor.
Add the eggs, bread crumbs, salt, and pepper; mix well.
In a large frying pan, heat enough oil to cover the bottom to a depth of at least an inch. Wet your hands and shape the mixture into ovals, and drop into hot oil.
Cook, turning, until both sides are browned. Drain well and serve hot.
Serves 4 to 6.

Cheddar Cheese Puff

Great for brunch—and so easy since you can start it the day before. This recipe is from Norene Gilletz's *Food Processor Bible*. Norene suggests that this dish not be frozen, and she gives low-fat suggestions.

8 ounces chilled cheddar cheese (2 cups grated)
6 slices stale bread (white, whole wheat, or challah), torn into chunks
2 tablespoons melted butter (optional)
3 eggs (or 2 eggs plus 2 egg whites)
1 teaspoon salt
1/4 teaspoon pepper
3/4 teaspoon dry mustard
2 cups milk (low-fat or regular)

Place the cheese into a greased 7x11-inch glass baking dish.
Using the food processor with the steel blade, drop bread chunks through the feed tube while the machine is running, processing to make bread crumbs.
Spread evenly over the cheese in the baking dish and drizzle with melted butter (if using).
Process eggs, salt, pepper, mustard, and milk for 5 seconds.
Immediately pour over bread/cheese mixture, cover with foil, and refrigerate for 1/2 hour or up to 24 hours.
Preheat oven to 350°F. Bake puff for 30 minutes, then uncover and bake 30 minutes longer, until nicely browned.
Serves 6 to 8.

To determine if an egg is fresh, place it in a glass of water. If it stands on the large end, it is stale. If it lies on its side, it is fresh. Always keep eggs covered in the refrigerator because they absorb odors.

Cherry and Goat Cheese Strudel

An unusual combination of ingredients makes this dessert from pastry chef David Becker a real winner.

3 ounces butter
1 ounce confectioners' sugar (2 & 1/2 tablespoons)
2 ounces fresh chopped mint
1 vanilla bean split and scraped or a teaspoon of vanilla
3 large egg yolks
12 ounces goat cheese
5 ounces mascarpone cheese
3 large egg whites
2 ounces sugar (4 tablespoons)
4 ounces dried cherries
1/2 cup plain dry bread crumbs
1 box phyllo, at room temperature
4 ounces butter, melted

In a mixer, cream together butter, sugar, mint, and vanilla.
Slowly add egg yolks one at a time, beating well after each addition.
Crumble cheese and drop into egg mixture, then add the mascarpone cheese, mixing well.
Whip whites to a stiff meringue along with the sugar. Fold meringue into the cheese mixture, then fold in the cherries and bread crumbs.
Preheat oven to 350°F. Place a sheet of phyllo on the counter with the long side parallel to you. Brush lightly with melted butter, place another sheet on top, brush, and repeat until you have used 5 sheets.
Brush the top sheet and spread 1/3 of the filling in a thin layer, covering the top sheet of phyllo, except for 3 inches at the top (away from you).
Be sure to spread it around evenly.
Starting with the edge closest to you, tightly roll up the phyllo and filling until you are 3 inches from the top edge. Fold the sides over towards the center, then finish rolling up the strudel.

Place on a jelly-roll pan, brush the top with butter, and repeat making 2 more strudels.

Bake them for 20 minutes or until golden brown. Let sit for a few minutes, then slice on the diagonal into serving pieces.

Makes 12 large servings.

Chicken and Pistachio Balls

Tired of meatballs? This alternative can be used as an appetizer or a main course and can be made ahead and/or frozen, fried, or broiled.

1 pound raw chicken breasts, minced/ground in food processor
1 large egg, lightly beaten
3/4 cup to 1 cup dry/stale bread crumbs from a stale baguette or French
    bread
1/2 cup shelled, chopped pistachio nuts (unsalted)
1/2 teaspoon ground turmeric, or more to taste
1/2 teaspoon ground cinnamon, or more to taste
1 teaspoon ground coriander, or more to taste
1/2 cup all-purpose flour
1/4 cup or more olive oil

In a large bowl, combine the chicken and the egg, then add the bread
    crumbs, nuts, and spices and mix well to combine.
Shape the mixture into golf-ball-size balls with your hands and roll lightly
in the flour. Shake off any excess flour.
Cover the bottom of a medium-size skillet with the oil and heat over medium high heat.
Add just enough balls so they are not touching or crowded.
Cook, turning, until browned on all sides and done in the middle. Remove from skillet and drain well on paper towels.
Add more oil if needed and cook the remaining chicken balls.
If you do not wish to cook them in oil, shape them into patties and do not
    dip them in the flour. Just broil them until done. They will not have
    the crisp coating, but will be just as delicious.
Makes about 14 balls.

 Herbs and spices will keep their flavor longer if they are stored away
    from heat (like the stove or oven).

Hazelnut Caramel Cake

For a treat on a festive day, Anne Willan makes this moist, rich cake with a topping of crisp caramel. Like most nut cakes, it improves when kept a day or two in an airtight container, but the topping should be added only a short time before serving as caramel softens after a few hours in the open air.

Cookbook author Anne Willan is also the founder and president of La Varenne Cooking School (www.lavarenne.com and www.chateau dufey.com). Her many books include *La Varenne Pratique, From My Chateau Kitchen*, and the *Look and Cook* collection with over seventeen volumes (the basis for the PBS series). Her most recent book, *A Cook's Book of Fixes and Kitchen Tips*, is an irresistible kitchen resource.

2 slices stale white bread
1 cup hazelnuts, toasted
pinch of salt
1/2 cup plus 2 tablespoons butter, more for the pan
2/3 cup sugar
4 large eggs, separated
grated zest of 1 lemon

Topping:
1/3 cup sugar
1/4 cup water
8 toasted hazelnuts

Heat the oven to 350°F. Butter a 9-inch cake pan, line it with a round of parchment paper and butter the paper.

Toast the bread in the oven until very dry, 6 to 8 minutes. Let it cool, leaving the oven on. Break the bread in pieces and grind it to crumbs in the food processor.

Add the hazelnut pieces and salt and grind to a coarse powder (the dry bread helps keep the nuts light).

Cream the butter in a mixer fitted with the whisk attachment.

Add half the sugar and continue beating until light and soft, 3 to 5 minutes.

Add the egg yolks, one by one, beating well after each addition.

Beat in the lemon zest. With a spoon, stir in the ground-nut mixture.

Using the mixer with another bowl, whisk the egg whites until stiff.

With the whisk turning, gradually add the remaining sugar and continue beating until this meringue is stiff and glossy, 30 seconds to 1 minute.

Stir about a quarter of the meringue into the nut mixture to lighten it, then add all the mixture to the remaining meringue.

Fold the two together as lightly as possible.

Spoon the batter into the cake pan and bake until the cake pulls from the sides of the pan and a skewer inserted in the center comes out clean when withdrawn, 40 to 50 minutes. Let the cake cool 5 minutes, then turn it out onto a rack covered with a sheet of parchment paper.

Strip the lining paper from the cake and leave it upside down (so it has a flat top) to cool completely, at least an hour.

For the topping, put the sugar and water in a small saucepan and heat gently without stirring until the sugar dissolves.

Raise the heat and boil until the sugar cooks to a golden brown caramel.

Turn the cake top upwards and set it back on the rack.

Take the caramel from the heat, let the bubbles subside and at once pour it over the cake, spreading with a metal spatula to make a very thin layer, letting it drip down the sides. Take care, as caramel can burn badly.

Decorate the cake at once with hazelnut halves so they stick to the caramel.

The caramel will become crisp as it cools. When starting to set, mark portions in the caramel with a knife so the cake is easy to cut in wedges.

Serves 6 to 8.

Heady Bread Pudding with Madeira Sauce

The Madeira sauce is what makes this rich bread pudding a little heady. If you don't have Madeira, try some dark rum or brandy. Scalding the half-and-half with the whole spices imparts a rich, lovely flavor and gives more aroma to the dish. However, if you don't have the whole spices, add a scant teaspoon of ground cinnamon and a generous 1/4 teaspoon of ground mace to the half-and-half (it isn't necessary to scald) and let it steep. This lovely recipe is from author and herb expert Susan Belsinger, who tells me she finds the pudding especially "toothsome" when she makes it with whole-wheat or whole-grain bread.

2 cups half-and-half
4-inch cinnamon stick
1/2 teaspoon mace blades
2 tablespoons unsalted butter
2 extra large eggs, beaten lightly
1/3 cup sugar
1/2 teaspoon pure vanilla extract
3 cups dry bread crumbs or approximately 3 slices of stale bread torn
    into bite size pieces
1/2 cup golden raisins soaked in 1/2 cup Madeira wine

Preheat the oven to 350°F. Butter a 1.5-quart baking dish.
In a medium-size saucepan, scald the half-and-half with the cinnamon
    and mace.
Stir the butter in until melted. Cool the mixture to lukewarm, then pour
    though a strainer.
Discard the spices.
Beat the eggs into the half-and-half. Stir in the sugar and vanilla and
    mix well.
Place the bread or bread crumbs in the buttered baking dish and pour the
    egg mixture over them.
Drain the raisins, reserving the Madeira. Lightly toss the raisins into the
    bread mixture with a fork.
Place the baking dish in a larger pan and fill the pan with hot water to
    come halfway up the sides of the dish.

Bake for about 45 minutes or until the custard is just set.

Remove the pudding from the hot water and let the pudding cool on a rack. The pudding is best served slightly warm or at room temperature, not hot or cold. Serve with the Madeira Wine Sauce or heavy cream.

Serves 6.

Madeira Wine Sauce

6 tablespoons unsalted butter
4 tablespoons light brown sugar
1 extra large egg
1/2 cup Madeira

Prepare the sauce by heating the butter and sugar in a small, heavy-bottomed saucepan over moderate heat, stirring constantly.

Beat the egg in a small bowl with a whisk. Pour about half of the butter and sugar mixture into the beaten egg and whisk until well blended.

Return to the saucepan and blend well. Gradually add the Madeira, whisking well after each addition.

Cook over medium-low heat, stirring frequently, until the sauce is thick and comes to a bare simmer. Do not allow the sauce to boil.

Serve hot, warm, or at room temperature. This can be made ahead and gently reheated. Makes about 1/2 cup.

Don't pre-measure vanilla or liquors until you are ready to add them to the recipe as they evaporate quickly.

Lemon-Baked Fish with Cranberry-Lemon Sauce

This lemony fish with stuffing is a lovely dish for company or family. The stuffing can be prepared in advance and the dish assembled right before baking. Just bring the stuffing to room temperature so the dish cooks evenly. The recipe is from Linda Wolfe's book *Old Orange Grove Recipes*.

1/2 cup chopped onion
1/2 cup chopped celery
6 tablespoons butter, divided
4 cups soft fresh bread crumbs
1 teaspoon salt
1 teaspoon grated lemon rind
1/4 cup lemon juice
2 pounds fish fillets
12 thin lemon slices

Preheat oven to 350°F.
In a medium skillet, sauté onion and celery in 4 tablespoons of the butter.
Add bread crumbs, salt, lemon rind, and lemon juice and pour stuffing mixture into a greased baking dish.
Arrange fish fillets on top. Drizzle remaining 2 tablespoons butter over fish.
Arrange lemon slices around fish fillets.
Bake for 25 to 30 minutes. When fish is done and flakes easily, serve.
Drizzle Cranberry-Lemon Sauce over portions as you serve them.
Serves 4.

 To cook fish properly, follow the "Ten Minute Rule." Measure the fish fillet or steak at its thickest part and allow ten minutes of cooking time per inch of thickness. If the fish measures less than 1-inch thick, shorten the cooking time slightly. To calculate the right amount of fish for serving, it is 1/3 to 1/2 pound per person for fillets or steaks; if the fish is whole it is 3/4 to 1 pound per person.

Cranberry-Lemon Sauce

1 tablespoon sugar
1 tablespoon cornstarch
10-ounce package frozen cranberries with orange
1/2 cup water
4 tablespoons lemon juice
1 teaspoon grated lemon rind

In a small saucepan cook sugar and cornstarch.
Add the package of cranberry-orange and remaining ingredients.
Cook until thick and clear, stirring constantly.

Lemony Cheese Custard Squares

In Spain this dessert is called *Quesada* and is more like a custard than a cheesecake. It is made with soft, fresh cheese, before the curds have been pressed or salted. These smooth lemony squares are especially good when served with fresh strawberries. This is another winner from Janet Mendel's *My Kitchen in Spain*.

4 to 5 slices stale bread, crusts removed
1 cup milk
1 teaspoon grated lemon zest
1-inch piece of cinnamon stick
3 tablespoons butter
3/4 cup sugar
3 large eggs
2 cups *fromage blanc* or other unsalted fresh cheese (like unsalted cottage cheese or well-drained yogurt)

Break the bread into pieces and pulse in a food processor until the bread is reduced to fine crumbs. There should be 1 & 1/2 cups of crumbs.

Remove 3 tablespoons of the crumbs and reserve in a small bowl. Leave rest of crumbs in the processor.

Combine the milk, lemon zest, and cinnamon stick in a small saucepan. Bring to a boil and remove from the heat. Let cool until lukewarm, then remove and discard the cinnamon.

Preheat oven to 375°F. Butter a 9x13-inch baking pan. Sprinkle with reserved bread crumbs.

Pour the milk over the bread crumbs in the food processor. Process until smooth.

Using an electric mixer, cream the butter in a mixing bowl at medium speed.

Gradually beat in the sugar, then the eggs, one at a time. Add the *fromage blanc* and combine well.

Stir in the bread and milk mixture from the processor.

Pour the batter into the pan. Bake until the custard is set and a skewer comes out clean, about 35 minutes.

Allow squares to cool in the pan. Loosen the edges and turn out onto a
  work surface.

Cut into rectangles or squares, about 3x2 inches.

Makes 18 squares.

 Lemons with the smoothest skin and the least points on the
ends have more juice and flavor.

Migas

The bread used in this recipe should be dense, a fine-textured country bread, baked in a round loaf, two days old. If this is not available, use a compact loaf of Italian-style bread.

According to Janet Mendel (in her book *My Kitchen in Spain*), this is the breakfast food for country people everywhere. *Migas* means "crumbs" and most versions are made with crumbled stale bread that has been fried up with bits of bacon or sausage and garlic, then served with an eclectic selection of accompaniments, including fresh grapes or raisins, raw scallions, canned or fresh sardines, pomegranates, radishes, and melon. They make a fine side dish for fried eggs. Author Clarissa Hyman describes *Migas* "as a comfort food at its most soulful. A sort of comfort food fry-up made with savory sourdough breadcrumbs, potatoes, bacon, garlic, and pimenton."

This simple, rural dish adapts itself to whatever is available. It reflects the importance of bread on the Spanish table and the reminder of times when a crumb, however stale, was never wasted.

8 ounces stale country or sourdough bread (8 slices)
1/3 cup olive oil
2 garlic cloves, quartered lengthwise
3 thick slices (or 3 ounces) lean bacon cut crosswise in strips (turkey bacon for kosher)
1/2 teaspoon salt
1 teaspoon pimenton or paprika*
pinch ground cumin
pinch ground cloves
pinch freshly ground black pepper
a few grapes or raisins

Cut the bread into 1/2-inch bits. You should have about 5 cups of bread cubes.
Place the diced bread in a bowl and sprinkle with 1/2 cup water.
Toss the bread bits until they are dampened, but not soaked. Place them on a dampened kitchen towel and wrap them tightly.
Let stand overnight or for at least 6 hours.

Heat the oil in a deep skillet over medium heat. Fry the pieces of garlic and strips of bacon until lightly browned, 3 to 4 minutes, then skim them out and reserve, keeping the bacon fat in the pan.

Add the bread bits to the pan. Fry the crumbs over medium heat, turning them constantly with a spatula. At first they will tend to stick to the skillet. Keep stirring until they are loose and lightly toasted, about 20 minutes. Keep cutting the bread with the edge of the spatula to gradually reduce the dice into crumbs.

Stir in the salt, pimenton, cumin, cloves, and pepper.

Return the fried garlic and bacon to the pan and give everything another few turns. The bread crumbs should be slightly crunchy, not crisp. Garnish with grapes or raisins.

Serves 4 as a side dish or 2 for breakfast.

* Pimenton is smoked Spanish paprika—it comes in three grades, *picante* (fiery), *dulce* (sweet), and *agridulce* (bittersweet)—but you can substitute any paprika.

Mushroom Sausage Strudel

I met Nina Claremont over twenty years ago when she was a well-known New York caterer who counted Al Pacino among her clients. She belonged to "The 99's," a women's flying club (formed with the first ninety-nine women pilots plus Amelia Earhart) along with my then-editor who introduced us. Our love of cooking and eating made us fast friends. This is one of the first recipes she shared with me.

4 tablespoons butter, or pareve margarine
1 medium onion, chopped
1 pound fresh mushrooms, wiped clean and chopped
salt
freshly ground pepper
1 pound raw meat sausage—preferably Italian (and as hot or mild as you like!)
1 pound box phyllo, at room temperature
1 cup melted butter or margarine
1 cup fine unseasoned dry breadcrumbs

Preheat oven to 350°F.
In a large skillet over medium heat, melt 4 tablespoons butter and sauté the chopped onion for 3 minutes.
Stir in the chopped mushrooms and salt and pepper to taste, mixing well.
Cook for a minute and mix in the sausage, stirring well. Cooking for a minute or two. Remove pan from heat.
Lay out the phyllo dough as directed on the package.
Grease or spray a large jelly-roll pan. Brush the melted butter on a sheet of phyllo and sprinkle it with bread crumbs.
Place another sheet of phyllo over the first one, brush with butter, and sprinkle with bread crumbs. Repeat this until you have done 5 layers.
Place the sausage mixture on top of the last layer and spread evenly over the phyllo, stopping one inch from all edges.
Roll the phyllo the long way, like a jelly roll. Brush the top and sides with the melted butter.
Cut diagonal slits an inch apart and about 1/2-inch deep in the top of the roll. Place strudel on the prepared sheet, and bake for 30 to 45

minutes. Remove from oven and cut slits through to the bottom of the strudel and serve hot.

If freezing, bake only for 15 to 20 minutes, cool to room temperature, wrap and freeze.

To reheat, bake frozen on a cookie sheet at 400°F until hot.

Serves 10 to 12.

Pistachio Nut Paté

This is filling, nutritious, and delicious. A wonderful vegetarian main course, which can also be served as an appetizer or a side dish. Usually, a paté is a pie or pastry containing meat. Or it can be a spread of mashed spiced meat.

3/4 cup celery, chopped fine
1/4 cup onion, chopped fine
2 tablespoons canola oil, divided plus 1 teaspoon butter
1/3 cup chopped walnuts or pecans
2/3 cup chopped almonds (or use one cup of chopped walnuts, pecans, or almonds)
1/4 cup chopped pistachio nuts
1 & 1/2 cups cottage cheese
1 cup dry bread crumbs
3 large eggs, beaten
1/2 teaspoon salt
1/2 teaspoon thyme or tarragon or any herb—or more to taste
9-inch pre-baked pie shell or 12 pre-baked 3-inch tart shells (optional)

Preheat oven to 350°F.

Sauté celery and onion in 1 tablespoon oil and butter in a large skillet, until softened (3 to 5 minutes). Add nuts and stir for another minute or two. Remove pan from heat, let cool for a minute or two.

Stir in cottage cheese, bread crumbs, eggs, 1 tablespoon oil, salt, and thyme, mixing well.

Pour into an 8-inch pan and bake for 45 to 60 minutes or until done. If you don't wish to make this as a paté, use the piecrust or tart shells. Serve hot, warm, or cold. If hot, sour cream is a nice sauce. Freezes beautifully.

Serves 8 to 10.

Red Pepper Spread (Muhammara)

This recipe is from Gaziantep in South Eastern Turkey, and appeared in the book I co-authored with Nur Ilkin, *A Taste of Turkish Cuisine*. Aleppo pepper flakes are available in Korean or Mediterranean markets.

1 cup Aleppo pepper
1 cup extra-virgin olive oil
1 cup stale bread crumbs (not canned)
1 cup ground walnuts
1 teaspoon sugar
3 to 4 garlic cloves, minced (using a garlic press)
salt
freshly ground pepper
1/2 teaspoon ground cumin
juice of 1/2 lemon

Soak the Aleppo pepper in 1/2 cup water and let it sit for 10 to 15 minutes or until all the water is absorbed and mixture has a paste-like consistency. Mix well.

Add the olive oil, bread crumbs, and walnuts, mixing well. Add the sugar, garlic, salt and pepper to taste, and cumin, mixing well. Add the lemon juice, mix well, taste, and adjust seasoning if needed.

Serve at room temperature with bread, crackers, or pita bread.

Makes 3 cups.

Rye and Whiskey Torte

There were a number of wonderful cake recipes in circulation when I got married, many, many years ago that used rye, pumpernickel, or other types of bread crumbs instead of flour. These light cakes had no butter or fat, were moist, and froze well. This is one of those recipes. It can be iced, topped with confectioners' sugar, or (after you remove it from the oven) sprinkled with a cup of chocolate chips. Then, using a metal spatula, immediately spread chips as they melt.

9 large eggs, separated
1 & 1/2 cup confectioners' sugar, sifted
2 cups coarse grated stale rye bread crumbs (crusts removed)
3 tablespoons whiskey
1 teaspoon baking powder
1 teaspoon cinnamon
1 teaspoon ground cloves
2 tablespoons slivered citron (usually used in fruitcakes) (optional)
1/2 cup ground blanched almonds
1 square (1 ounce) unsweetened chocolate, grated

Preheat oven to 350°F. Grease a 9-inch spring form pan and set aside.

In the mixer, on medium speed, beat the egg yolks until thick and lemon colored, about 5 to 8 minutes.

Gradually add sugar and mix well.

Place the bread crumbs in a medium-size bowl and pour the whiskey over the crumbs and mix well (I use my fingers).

In another bowl, combine the baking powder, cinnamon, cloves, citron if using, almonds, and grated chocolate. Fold into the egg mixture along with the bread crumbs. Be sure mixture is well incorporated into the batter.

In a clean mixing bowl, beat the egg whites until soft peaks form and whites are stiff. Using a rubber spatula, fold whites into cake batter.

Pour into prepared pan and bake for 45 minutes or until cake tests done. Ice if desired.

Serves 10.

Salmon Loaf en Croute with Cucumber Dill Sauce or Yogurt Cucumber Sauce/Salad

The recipe is from Susie Fishbein's book *The Kosher Palette*. It is elegant and easy to prepare using common ingredients. In addition, I have given you my popular Yogurt and Cucumber Salad, known as *Tsatsiki* to use as an alternative sauce.

16-ounce can red or pink salmon, boned, skinned, and drained
3/4 cup dry bread crumbs from a stale baguette or French bread
3/4 cup mayonnaise
1/2 cup chopped yellow onions
1/2 teaspoon salt
freshly ground pepper
3 drops hot sauce (optional)
1/2 (17.3-ounce package) frozen puff pastry, thawed
1 large egg, lightly beaten

Preheat oven to 350°F. In a large bowl, combine the salmon, bread crumbs, mayonnaise, onion, salt, pepper, and hot sauce if using. Mix well.

Lightly flour a work surface and place the puff pastry on it. Gently roll it lengthwise and width-wise, stretching it a little. Turn so pastry is vertical, with short side (bottom) facing you.

Gently spoon the salmon mixture in a column down the middle section of the puff pastry.

Fold the right side over the salmon mixture, then the left side, overlapping puff pastry. Seal edges and carefully lift or roll onto an ungreased 9x3-inch cookie sheet, seam side down.

Brush the pastry with the egg and bake for about 45 minutes or until pastry is golden brown.

Serves 6.

Cucumber Dill Sauce

1 large cucumber, seeded and diced
3/4 cup mayonnaise
3 tablespoons chopped onion
1 tablespoon chopped fresh dill or 1 teaspoon dried dill
1/2 cup water

Combine cucumber, mayonnaise, onion, and dill in a medium-size bowl. Gradually add enough water to desired consistency; cover and chill. Serve in a small dish or in a fresh lemon basket. Yield: 1 & 1/2 cups.

Yogurt Cucumber Sauce/Salad
(Sephardic Israeli Cuisine)

1 large English cucumber, peeled, seeded, and sliced in half lengthwise
1/2 to 1 tablespoon sea salt, or to taste
1 & 1/4 cups strained yogurt
2 tablespoons extra virgin olive oil
1 tablespoon fresh lemon juice
freshly ground pepper, preferably white
2 to 4 large cloves of garlic, minced (or to taste)
1/4 cup fresh mint leaves (optional)
2 tablespoons chopped fresh parsley (optional)

Cut the cucumber into julienne pieces (matchstick size) or dice. Sprinkle with salt and place in a large colander and let it sit for an hour (to drain). In a large bowl, combine the yogurt, olive oil, lemon juice, pepper, and garlic.

Mix well, cover and refrigerate until serving. Before serving, using a wooden spoon, "beat" the yogurt sauce until smooth. Cut or tear the mint into small pieces if using. Dry the cucumber pieces by squeezing them in paper towels to remove all of the water.

Stir the pieces of cucumber into the yogurt mixture. Add the mint (and parsley if using) and mix well to combine. Add salt and pepper to taste, mix well.

Serves 6 to 8.

Sherron's Onion Strudel

Sherron Goldstein and I met in a cooking class when she was visiting Maryland. Our love of cooking and eating created an instant bond, and later she invited me to Birmingham, Alabama, to teach at her cooking school. Her book *Fresh Fields* offers a variety of wonderful recipes, and this is one of them.

4 medium red onions, sliced
3 tablespoons butter or margarine
2 tablespoons flour
freshly ground pepper to taste
3/4 cup vegetable broth
1/4 cup white wine
1 & 1/2 cup toasted dry bread crumbs
1 cup shredded Swiss cheese
3 tablespoons grated Parmesan cheese
1 box phyllo pastry, defrosted, at room temperature
1 cup melted butter
1/4 cup yellow cornmeal

Preheat oven to 350°F. Cover a jelly-roll pan with parchment paper.
Sauté onions in 3 tablespoons butter in a skillet until tender. Stir in the flour and pepper and mix in the broth and white wine. Cook over medium heat until thick and bubbly, whisking constantly.
Let mixture stand until cool, then stir in the bread crumbs and Swiss and Parmesan cheese.
Place 6 sheets of phyllo on a work surface and cover with a damp towel to prevent drying out. Brush 1 sheet at a time with melted butter and sprinkle lightly with cornmeal, stacking one on top of another after completion of each sheet.
With long side of phyllo stack facing you, spread 1/2 of onion mixture along the bottom 1/3 (of the top sheet) leaving a 1-inch border on all sides.
Fold the sides (ends) over onion mixture and then roll as a jelly roll.
Place seam side down on baking sheet, brush roll with additional butter.
Repeat process with 6 more pieces of phyllo, onion mixture, and melted

butter to make another strudel. Bake at 350°F for 35 to 45 minutes or until golden brown.

Serves 6 to 8.

 To keep cheeses fresh, cover them with a cloth moistened in vinegar or store the cheese, grated, in a tightly covered jar in the refrigerator.

Snappy Bread Pudding

This wonderful cold-weather dessert enables you to use up stale bread while insuring that your family gets a nutritious dessert.

butter for greasing
1/2 cup golden raisins
1/4 cup rum
4 large eggs
1 cup sugar
pinch of salt
1/2 teaspoon nutmeg
1/2 easpoon cinnamon
1 tablespoon vanilla
1 tablespoon rum (optional)
4 cups milk, scalded
4 cups stale bread crumbs

Preheat oven to 325°F. Grease a 2-quart casserole.

In a small bowl, soak the raisins in the rum for about 15 minutes. Drain raisins and set aside.

In a large bowl, beat the eggs until foamy. Add the sugar, salt, spices, vanilla, and rum, beating well. Gradually stir in the scalded milk.

Add the bread cubes to the bowl, mixing until they are well saturated with the liquid.

Add the raisins. Pour mixture into the prepared casserole.

Bake for 1 & 1/4 to 1 & 1/2 hours, or until a knife inserted in the center comes out clean.

Cool the pudding on a wire rack for 30 minutes before serving.

Serve warm with whipped cream or vanilla ice cream, if desired.

Serves 8.

Thick Spaghetti with Bread Crumbs

This interesting, delicious combination of spaghetti, toasted bread crumbs, and sugar is a favorite of Mary Ann Esposito, creator and host of the PBS cooking series *Cio Italia*. This is from her book, *Mangia Pasta! Perciatelli*. It is similar to spaghetti, but thicker and hollow, and is also called *bucatini*. A coarse-type bread makes the best crumbs; soft bread does not have enough texture and crunch to hold up when tossed with the cooked pasta. Great as a first course.

6 tablespoons extra virgin olive oil
1 & 1/2 cups coarse dry bread crumbs
1 tablespoon sugar
1 pound perciatelli or spaghetti
1 & 1/2 teaspoons fine sea salt

In a large skillet, heat 2 tablespoons of the olive oil. Add the bread crumbs and stir with a wooden spoon to coat them with the oil.
Cook the crumbs over medium heat, stirring occasionally, until they are golden brown in color.
Remove the crumbs to a bowl, stir in the sugar, and set aside.
Cook the perciatelli according to package instructions, drain well but reserve 2 tablespoons of the cooking water.
Return the pasta to the cooking pot, stir in the water, the remaining 1/4 cup olive oil, and the salt.
Transfer the pasta to a platter and sprinkle half of the bread crumbs over the top. Toss pasta with 2 spoons to evenly coat the strands with the crumbs.
Sprinkle remaining crumbs over the top and serve immediately.
Serves 4 to 6.

Turkey "Meatballs" with Cashew Nuts

I usually don't like meatballs since I find them too dry, but a friend raved about these, and I decided to try them. She was right; they are great! They freeze well and can be used as an appetizer or a main course.

1 pound ground turkey

2 teaspoons + 1 tablespoon soy sauce

1 large egg

1 teaspoon dry white sherry (optional) + 2 tablespoons dry white sherry (optional)

1/4 cup dry bread crumbs

2 scallions, chopped

9 ounces Hoisin sauce, divided

1/3 cup chopped raw cashews

1 cup apple juice

1 tablespoon sesame oil

2 tablespoons sherry (optional)

1 teaspoon grated fresh ginger

In a large bowl, combine the turkey, 2 teaspoons soy sauce, egg, 1 teaspoon sherry if using, bread crumbs, scallions, 3 ounces Hoisin sauce, and cashews. Mix well.

Using your hands, make "meatballs" the size of walnuts and set aside.

In a large pot, bring the remaining 1 tablespoon soy sauce, Hoisin sauce, apple juice, sesame oil, remaining 2 tablespoons sherry if using, and grated ginger to a boil. Reduce heat to simmer and cook for approximately 20 minutes or until browned and the sauce begins to thicken. If serving as a main course, serve with rice.

Serves 4 as a main course, more as an appetizer.

Zucchini Delights

A versatile vegetable dish that goes with anything, doubles easily, and freezes beautifully. A great way to get your family to eat vegetables!

canola spray or butter for greasing
3 ounces grated Mozzarella cheese
2 cups unpeeled zucchini, grated (about 1 large zucchini)
1/2 small onion, minced
2 large eggs, lightly beaten
salt
freshly ground pepper
1/2 cup fresh bread crumbs

Preheat oven to 375°F. Grease 6 to 12 muffin tins (depends on how much of the mixture you put in each tin). In a large bowl, combine all the ingredients, mixing well.
Pour batter into prepared muffin cups and bake for 25 to 30 minutes.
Serve hot. To freeze, cool completely, wrap, and freeze.
Makes 6 to 12.

Bread Salads

Although the word "salad" usually calls to mind images of crisp greens, there are many cultures that relish cold dishes in which the primary ingredient is bread. In the Tuscany region of Italy, *Panzanella*, for example, a simple mixture of bread, tomatoes, cucumber or onion, and oil and vinegar, was known as a poor man's salad. This delicious and refreshing dish sustained many generations of Italian peasants. On this side of the Atlantic, that humble mélange has morphed into Tuscan Salad, and it can be found at the trendiest restaurants.

Although bread might form the base of such salads, the freshness of the other ingredients is still of prime importance. Summer, when fresh produce is in abundance, offers a wonderful opportunity to experiment with this delicious and hearty type of salad. It is also essential to start with a good-quality, firm Italian or French bread. If you remember that the dish will only be as good as the bread you put into it, you will be ready to take a crack at the wonderful variety of salad recipes that feature the "staff of life."

Bread Salad with Tuna and Capers

This dish combines two Tuscan favorites, tuna salad and *Panzanella*, a bread salad moistened with garden vegetables and olive oil. Sharon Sanders, who lived and loved in Italy, shared this recipe with me. It's from her book, *Cooking Up an Italian Life: Simple Pleasures of Italy in Recipe and Stories*.

8 to 10 ounces rustic stale bread, cut into 1/2-inch slices
1 bunch scallions, white and green parts, chopped
3 to 4 tablespoons red or white wine vinegar
1/2 teaspoon salt
1/2 cup extra-virgin olive oil (approximately)
12-ounce can water-packed tuna, drained and flaked
1 large tomato, cut into thin wedges
2 ribs celery hearts, sliced (optional)
3 to 4 tablespoons drained capers

Toast the bread. Cut into 1/2-inch cubes; set aside. Reserve 2 tablespoons of the dark green scallion stems.
In a large bowl, whisk the vinegar and salt. Add the oil and whisk to combine.
Add the tuna, tomato, all the chopped scallions except reserved stems, celery, 3 tablespoons capers, and bread.
Toss and set aside for 15 to 30 minutes at room temperature. Toss occasionally.
Taste a bread cube. If it seems too dry, drizzle with a bit more oil or a few tablespoons of cold water. If too bland, add up to 1 tablespoon vinegar and 1 tablespoon capers. Sprinkle each serving with scallion stems
Serves 4 to 6.

Cornbread Salad

This salad is as delicious to eat as it is beautiful to look at. "Sweet with a kick" best describes this recipe from Sherron Goldstein, a well-known Birmingham, Alabama, author and cooking teacher. By using cornbread, she adds a definite Southern flair to this Italian bread salad. The salad mixture can be made early in the day, covered, and refrigerated. The dressing can also be made ahead, covered, and refrigerated separately.

3 cups, 1/2-inch diced stale cornbread*
1 cucumber, seeded and diced
1 large tomato, seeded and diced
1/2 cup red bell pepper, diced
1/2 cup yellow bell pepper, diced
1/4 cup finely diced red onion
1/4 cup thinly sliced green onions
2 garlic cloves, finely chopped
1/4 cup white wine vinegar
1/3 cup extra virgin olive oil
1 teaspoon (canned) chipotle chili in adobe sauce (this is spicy!) coarsely
    chopped (optional)
1 tablespoon honey
1/4 cup chopped cilantro
salt
freshly ground pepper

Preheat oven to 350°F. Spread cornbread in an even layer on a baking
    sheet and bake for 20 minutes, or until crispy.
In a large bowl, place cucumber, tomato, yellow and red bell peppers, red
    onion, green onion, and garlic. Toss to mix well. Add cornbread cubes
    and lightly toss to mix.
In a small bowl, combine the wine vinegar, olive oil, chipotle chili, honey,
    cilantro, and salt and pepper to taste to make the vinaigrette.
Pour vinaigrette over salad ingredients and toss to mix well. Let stand 15
    to 30 minutes so bread can absorb the dressing, then serve.
Serves 4 to 6.

*If your cornbread is fresh, cut it in 1/2-inch cubes then proceed as directed. If your cornbread is 2- to 3-inches thick, cut it in half horizontally before proceeding. Lay slabs of bread on a cookie sheet and carefully slice parallel lines 1/2-inch apart in bread. Bake for 10 minutes, cut bread into 1/2-inch pieces, turn them over, and bake another 10 minutes or until pieces are firm, or golden brown.

Fresh tomatoes keep longer if stored with the stems down on the counter, do not refrigerate them. Tomatoes cut vertically "bleed" less.

Fettush Salad

Fettush is a Lebanese and northern Israeli salad made with roughly cut tomatoes, green bell peppers, onions, scallions, fresh mint, parsley, and watercress, or any wild green in bloom. The dressing is made with lemon juice, garlic, and olive oil. At first it sounds like any Israeli salad, but the addition of pita bread brushed with olive oil, sprinkled with *za'atar*, and baked until crisp adds to the texture and flavor of this Arabic version of Caesar Salad. Fettush was created as a way to use up day-old bread (since bread is not baked every day during Ramadan), by soaking it in dressing and serving it with vegetables to break the daily fast. This recipe is from Joan Nathan's book, *The Foods of Israel Today*.

2 whole pita breads
3 tablespoons extra virgin olive oil
1 teaspoon *za'atar*, or to taste (see below or available in Mediterranean and Middle Eastern markets, or some gourmet shops)
2 tomatoes, diced
1 green bell pepper, diced
1 cucumber, diced
1/2 medium onion, cut into 1-inch chunks
2 scallions, white and green, chopped
1 cup watercress or any wild greens
1/4 cup coarsely chopped fresh mint
1/4 cup coarsely chopped fresh cilantro or parsley
1 clove garlic, minced
2 tablespoons lemon juice
1 teaspoon salt, or to taste
1/4 teaspoon freshly ground pepper, or to taste

Za'atar

1/4 cup dried oregano and thyme, crumbled
2 tablespoons dried sumac (available in Mediterranean and Middle Eastern markets)
1/4 cup roasted sesame seeds
salt to taste
Mix za'atar ingredients well in a bowl. Makes 3/4 cup.

Preheat the oven to 350°F.

Brush the pita breads with 1 tablespoon of the olive oil and sprinkle with 1/2 teaspoon of *za'atar*. Bake on a cookie sheet for about 5 minutes or until crisp but not browned.

Place the vegetables in a salad bowl. Add the scallions, watercress, mint, and cilantro and toss together.

Put the garlic, lemon juice, salt, and pepper in a small bowl. Whisk in the remaining olive oil.

Just before serving, pour the dressing over the vegetables and sprinkle with the remaining *za'atar*. Break up the pita and toss gently with the vegetables. Adjust seasonings and serve immediately.

Serves 4 to 6.

Citrus fruits yield nearly twice the amount of juice if they are dropped into hot water for a few minutes before you squeeze them, or roll them back and forth beneath your hand on the counter top, or heat for ten seconds in the microwave.

Lebanese Bread Salad

This is a favorite recipe of my friend Jacquelyn Pickett and her husband. They first tasted it when a Lebanese friend made it. It was "love at first taste." The flavors get better if you allow this salad to sit overnight, but it does not keep well as a leftover.

1 small red or green pepper, diced
1/2 cucumber, peeled, seeded, and diced
1 cup chopped scallions
1/2 cup chopped red onion
1/2 cup chopped flat leaf parsley
1/4 cup chopped fresh mint
2 garlic cloves, crushed
1/4 cup fresh lemon juice
1/3 cup extra virgin olive oil
1 & 1/2 teaspoons sumac (available at Middle Eastern markets or Penzeys
     online catalog)
1/2 teaspoon salt
1/4 teaspoon pepper
4 medium tomatoes, peeled, seeded, diced
2 pita breads, split, toasted, and broken into 1/2-inch pieces

In a large bowl, combine everything except tomatoes. Bread must be added
     last.
Toss to mix well, cover, and refrigerate three hours or overnight.
Just before serving, add tomatoes and bread and toss well.
Serves 6 to 8.

Mediterranean Bread Salad

Using such staples as pita bread and feta cheese, this salad has a decidedly Greek accent. The addition of protein-rich chickpeas makes this a satisfying meatless main dish.

1 large red bell pepper
1 large pita (or other Middle Eastern flatbread)
1/2 cup + 1 tablespoon olive oil, divided
1 garlic clove, minced
1/4 cup chopped Italian (flat leaf) parsley
1/4 cup chopped fresh mint
1/4 cup chopped fresh basil
1/3 cup fresh lemon juice
1 cup finely chopped romaine lettuce
1 large cucumber, peeled, seeded and diced
1 (14-ounce) can chickpeas (garbanzo beans), drained
2 ripe tomatoes, chopped
1/2 cup chopped scallions
salt
freshly ground pepper
2/3 cup crumbled feta cheese

Preheat oven to broil.
Place pepper on a foil-lined baking sheet and broil 4 inches from heat source for 15 minutes, turning once or twice, until blackened on all sides.
Remove from oven and let stand in paper bag for 15 to 20 minutes; leave broiler on. When pepper is cool enough to handle, remove outer skin and seeds. Cut into small strips and set aside.
Meanwhile, brush pita with 1 tablespoon of olive oil, place on foil-lined baking sheet and broil about 5 inches from heat, turning once, until edges begin to curl and bread is firm. Let cool and then break into 1/2-inch pieces.
In a small bowl, combine garlic, parsley, mint, basil, and lemon juice.
Slowly whisk in remaining olive oil until smooth.

In large bowl, toss together lettuce, cucumber, pepper strips, chickpeas, tomatoes, and scallions. Add dressing, tossing to coat well.

Add pita bread pieces, season with salt and pepper to taste, and toss again. Top with feta cheese.

Serves 4 to 6 as a side dish, 3 to 4 as a main dish.

Panzanella

Panzanella, one of Tuscany's great salads, is a simple marriage of day-old bread, tomatoes, cucumber or onion, and oil and vinegar. Sometimes referred to as a poor man's salad, or summer salad, it sustained many generations of Italian peasants. Variations of this salad call for fresh basil leaves. For an easy warm-weather entrée, toss in strips of grilled chicken breast just before serving.

1 loaf stale firm, country-style bread
1 & 1/4 cups water
9 ripe tomatoes, diced
1 large red onion, diced
4 garlic cloves, minced
1 cup chopped Italian (flat leaf) parsley or 1/2 cup sliced basil leaves
1 & 1/2 tablespoons chopped fresh rosemary (or 1 teaspoon dried)
3 tablespoons extra-virgin olive oil
1/2 tablespoon red wine vinegar
1 teaspoon salt
1/4 teaspoon freshly ground pepper

Cut bread into large chunks and place in large bowl. Toss with water to moisten it completely and let stand 10 minutes. Squeeze out excess water, and coarsely chop bread into smaller cubes.

Place in bowl, and toss with tomatoes, onion, garlic, parsley, and rosemary.

In a small bowl, whisk together olive oil, vinegar, salt, and pepper and toss into salad, blending well.

Serves 6 to 8.

Tuscan Salad with Cucumber

This recipe differs from the more traditional versions because the bread cubes are baked into croutons. It also uses the small, tasty pickling cucumbers, which have fewer seeds.

1/2 cup olive oil, divided
1/2 loaf stale crusty Italian bread, cut into 1/2-inch cubes
salt
freshly ground pepper
6 pickling cucumbers
1 small red onion, thinly sliced
3 ripe tomatoes, diced
1/4 cup pitted green olives, halved
1/4 cup red wine vinegar
1 cup chopped Italian (flat leaf) parsley

Heat 1/4 cup olive oil in a large skillet over medium heat.
When oil is hot, add bread cubes and season with salt and pepper.
Reduce heat to low and cook, stirring frequently, until croutons are golden-brown and crisp. Remove from heat and let cool.
Peel cucumbers and cut into 1/2-inch chunks. Place in salad bowl with onions, tomatoes, and olives. Add vinegar, remaining oil, and parsley, along with additional salt and pepper to taste. Toss well and refrigerate 30 minutes. Add bread cubes, toss again and serve at once.
Serves 6.

Bread Soups

"Soup is cuisine's kindest course, it breathes re-assurance; it steams consolation; after a weary day it promotes sociability . . . there is nothing like a bowl of hot soup, its wisps of aromatic steam making the nostrils quiver with anticipation."

—Louis P. DeGroup *The Soup Book* (1949)

*S*oups—the most versatile and variable food—are synonymous with good eating and satisfying nourishment. Soups may be hot, cold, thick or thin, jellied, pureed, creamed, clear, or full of chunky pieces of meat and vegetables. In many parts of the world, in many cultures, a hot bowl of soup is a meal; in others, a remedy for illness.

Webster defines soup as a "liquid food" and as a word of Germanic origin (from *sop*, meaning the bread over which a pottage, broth, or other liquid was poured).

Grimod de la Reyniere said of soup, "It is to a dinner what a portico or a peristyle is to a building; that is to say, it's not only the first part of it, but must be devised in such a manner as the overture of an opera announces the subject of the work."

Soup's history is hard to trace, but ancient man apparently first made soup when he discovered the idea of filling an empty animal skin bag with meat, bones, and liquid, along with hot stones to cook the mixture. Ever since then, hearty soups have been the mainstay of family and communal meals.

An interesting recipe dating from the Middle Ages for *Soupe Au Pain* (bread soup) illustrates soup's long history: the soup is prepared by "making a cullis of sugar and white wine, ornamented with the yolks of eggs and perfumed with a few drops of rose water. Then toaste lightly a few slices of bread, cut rather thick, and toss them into the broth. When they are well saturated, dip them in a bath of hot oil. Then plunge them again into the broth, sprinkle them with sugar and saffron and serve at once." (Taillevant—as written in *Stews, Soups, and Chowders*, by Sheilah Kaufman.)

Always popular, soups can serve as a first course for a fancy dinner or as a hearty meal-in-a-bowl. Traditionally, soups have allowed cooks through the ages to use up the last handfuls of vegetables and snippets of meat, as well as providing a use for leftover bread in the form of croutons or crumbs. Soup preparation allows for imagination, creativity, and flexibility, and is one of the most forgiving dishes a cook can prepare. The recipes here all include bread in the making—but remember, too, that a slice of special bread on the side can be the perfect accompaniment to many other kinds of soup.

Essential Hints for Preparing Soup

The fresher and finer the ingredients, the better the soup.

Taste the soup often to achieve the right flavor, but let hot soup cool in the spoon before tasting it to get the real flavor.

Chilling soups will tone down the flavor, so taste it before serving and adjust the seasoning if needed.

Cold soups will be thicker after chilling.

Simmer means the slowest bubbling possible; next comes slow boil (a little faster); then boil, and then rapid boil (where you cook as quickly as possible).

Almond Soup

I was introduced to Cream of Almond Soup at my first French cooking class almost forty years ago. As I began to travel, I found a number of different soups, both hot and cold, that used almonds. This is a Spanish version adapted from Janet Mendel's *My Kitchen in Spain*.

3 tablespoons olive oil
1 cup blanched, skinned almonds
3 to 4 garlic cloves cut in half
2 cups diced stale white bread, crusts removed
6 cups chicken broth or stock (low fat is fine), divided
a pinch of saffron threads, crushed
freshly ground pepper
salt
2 teaspoons good quality white wine vinegar (Spanish or Italian)
chopped parsley, for garnish

Heat the oil in a 4- to 5-quart pot over medium heat.
Add the almonds, garlic, and diced bread and stir constantly for 1 to 3 minutes or until they are golden.
Remove pot from the heat and remove the almonds, garlic, and bread, leaving any remaining oil behind in the pot. Reserve 1/2 cup of the bread.
Place the remaining bread, almonds, garlic, a cup of the broth, saffron, pepper, salt, and the vinegar in the food processor with the metal knife blade and process for a few minutes until a smooth thick paste is formed.
Place the remaining broth in the pot and stir in the almond paste. Cook, stirring, until soup comes to a boil, then reduce heat and simmer for 15 minutes. Garnish with parsley and reserved bread crumbs.
Serves 6.

When a recipe calls for blanched almonds, save money by purchasing whole, unblanched almonds, which are less costly per pound. To remove the skins, simply pour boiling water over the almonds and let stand for 30 seconds. Drain off the water and the almond skins will slide right off. Then chop, sliver, or toast depending on the recipe.

Bread and Garlic Soup
a la Taberna del Alabardero

Called *Sopa de Ajo y Pan*, this recipe is common in Spain and is a great way of using day-old bread in a dish that is hearty and healthy. It is also looked at (and eaten) as a Spanish version of "chicken soup," since it's usually eaten when you are sick with the flu or on a cold winter day. This version is from Executive Chef Santi Zabaleta of Taberna del Alabardero, a restaurant in Washington, D.C. Now celebrating its fifteenth anniversary, Taberna del Alabardero has been designated by the Spanish Government as the "best Spanish restaurant outside of Spain" and received recognition as one of the best restaurants in the country by *Washingtonian* magazine, *Gourmet* magazine, the *New York Times*, and *Condé Nast Traveler*. The restaurant attracts luminaries ranging from royalty to rockers.

2 tablespoons extra virgin olive oil
8 cloves of garlic, sliced
1 tablespoon sweet paprika
1 stale loaf baguette bread (10 ounces) or white bread with crusts, cut in
    1/2 x 1/2-inch cubes
2 & 1/2 quarts chicken stock
salt to taste
2 large eggs, beaten

Heat the oil in a 4-quart stockpot and sauté the garlic. Before the garlic is completely golden, add the sweet paprika and the bread to the pot.
Slowly add the stock to stockpot, bring mixture to a light simmer, and continue to simmer uncovered for 30 to 45 minutes. Season with salt to taste. Bring soup to a boil. Once boiling, add the beaten eggs and bring back to a simmer for 5 minutes. Soup will resemble Egg-drop Soup.
Serves 4 to 6.

Chilled White Gazpacho
with Almonds and Grapes

This seductive blend of garlic, almonds, sherry vinegar, and ice water goes back a thousand years to the Moorish occupation of Spain. This version comes from Malaga, where it's garnished with sweet muscat grapes (use whatever sweet green grapes you can find).

This recipe is from *From Tapas to Meze: Small Plates from the Mediterranean*, by Joanne Weir, and she says, "In my estimation, *ajo blanco*, the Spanish white garlic soup, has never received its due. Traditionally a noon meal for peasants, it was prepared in the fields in a wooden bowl and eaten directly from the bowl with wooden spoons. Don't be afraid to add enough vinegar and salt to make the soup well balanced.

3/4 cup almonds, blanched
3 cloves garlic, peeled
1/2 teaspoon salt plus additional salt if needed
4 slices stale rustic country-style bread, crusts removed, about 4 ounces
4 cups ice water
5 tablespoons extra-virgin olive oil, divided
2 to 3 tablespoons white wine vinegar
2 tablespoons sherry vinegar
1 tablespoon unsalted butter
6 thick slices rustic country-style bread, crusts removed, cut in cubes, about 6 ounces
1 & 1/2 cups seedless green grapes

In a food processor, pulverize the almonds, 2 of the garlic cloves, and 1/2 teaspoon salt.
Soak the stale bread in 1 cup of the ice water and squeeze to extract the moisture. Discard the water. Add the bread to the food processor.
With the motor running, add 4 tablespoons of the olive oil and 1 cup of the ice water slowly in a steady stream.
Add the vinegars and mix on high speed until very smooth, 1 minute.
Add another 1 cup of the ice water and mix for 2 more minutes.

Place the soup in a bowl, add the remaining 1 cup ice water, and mix well. Season with additional salt and vinegar, if needed. Chill.

The soup can be prepared to this point and chilled up to 6 hours before serving.

Preheat the oven to 400°F. Melt the butter and heat the remaining 1 tablespoon olive oil in a frying pan over medium heat.

Crush the remaining garlic clove and add to the pan, stirring until golden. Remove and discard the garlic.

Add the bread, tossing to coat with the butter and oil, and place on a baking sheet. Bake, stirring occasionally, until the bread cubes are golden and crispy (about 12 to 15 minutes).

Serve the soup ice cold, garnished with the toasted bread cubes and grapes. *Serves 6.*

 To make your own wine vinegar from leftover wines that have begun to turn sour, add 2 tablespoons of red wine vinegar to 1 cup red wine or 2 tablespoons of white wine vinegar to 1 cup of white wine. Let stand, uncovered, at room temperature for 36 hours. Store in a jar with a tight-fitting lid.

Creamy Garlic Soup

In Italy, there are a number of rustic soups made by farm workers or laborers who would never throw bread away; so they made soups with chunks or pieces of bread. According to Lynne Rossetto Kasper in *The Italian Country Table*, "Farm women still revive a several-day old loaf that's beginning to dry up . . . and all over central and southern Italy, cooks simmer hard stale bread with water, salt, garlic and hot pepper, finishing the dish with olive oil . . . this is a soup—a good soup at that."

She also describes this custom: "when a piece of bread falls on the floor, it is immediately picked up and kissed in apology. In Puglia, it's bad luck if a dropped loaf of bread lands upside down. And the number of bread crumbs you drop predicts the number of years you'll spend in purgatory."

This recipe is a favorite of David P. Martone, CCP, cooking teacher and owner of the cooking school/shop Classic Thyme, in New Jersey.

6 cups stale Italian Bread, cut in 1-inch cubes
12 medium cloves garlic, peeled
4 tablespoons olive oil (more if needed)
1 to 2 teaspoons hot paprika (to taste and degree of heat desired)
1/2 cup dry sherry
8 cups chicken stock
salt
freshly ground pepper
fresh chopped parsley or herbs to garnish

Heat the oil in a large stockpot over medium heat.
Add the garlic and sauté until golden. Add the bread and sauté until golden.
Add the paprika and stir well to coat bread. Add the sherry to deglaze the
    pan. Start adding the chicken stock. Bring to a simmer and cook,
    uncovered, for 30 minutes.
With an immersion blender puree the soup, adjust seasoning, and serve
    topped with chopped herbs.
For an added treat, drizzle some extra-virgin olive oil on top before
    serving.
Serves 6 to 8.

Fresh garlic keeps until it turns soft, shrivels up, or sends out green shoots. It is stored best whole, in bulbs, in a cool, dry place. Do not seal it in a container or store it in the refrigerator (since the flavor will diminish). If the garlic bulb is fresh, plump, and firm when you buy it, it should stay fresh for more than a month.

Roasted Tomato Bread Soup

When I told Susie Fishbein about this book and asked if she had anything that would "fit," she exclaimed, "Oh, I have a fabulous Roasted Tomato Bread Soup." So here it is. From her book, *Kosher By Design Entertains* (Mesorah Publications).

1 large stale loaf (about 15-inches long) rustic bread, preferably Portu-
    guese, French, or Italian bread
1/4 cup extra-virgin olive oil plus 1 tablespoon
salt
freshly ground black pepper
2 garlic cloves, minced
6 whole plum tomatoes
3 garlic cloves, sliced
2 medium shallots, peeled and sliced
28-ounce can whole peeled tomatoes
6 cups chicken or vegetable broth
1 tablespoon chopped chives
1 tablespoon Italian flat leaf parsley, cut into thin ribbons

Preheat oven to 350°F.
Using a serrated knife, trim the crusts off the bread. Cut the bread into
    1-inch cubes and place on a baking sheet. Drizzle with 1/4 cup olive
    oil and season with salt, pepper, and minced garlic. Toss to coat
    evenly.
Toast the bread until it is hard and crunchy, like croutons, about 20 min-
    utes, stirring every 5 minutes so all sides are toasted. Remove from
    the oven and set aside.
Turn the oven to broil.
Cut the plum tomatoes in half and scoop out and discard the seeds. Place
    the tomato halves cut side down on a baking sheet. Broil until black-
    ened and the skin blistered, about 8 to 10 minutes.
Meanwhile, heat a tablespoon of olive oil in a medium or large soup pot.
    Add the sliced garlic and shallots and sauté over medium heat until
    shiny, about 4 to 5 minutes.

Add the can of tomatoes with the liquid. Break the tomatoes with the back of your spoon.

Add in half of the toasted bread cubes and simmer for 10 minutes.

Remove and discard the blackened tomato skins. Add the roasted tomatoes to the pot.

Add the broth and simmer for 5 minutes. Add the chives and parsley. Mix well.

Puree the soup using an immersion blender in the pot, or transfer in batches to a blender. Puree for 3 to 4 full minutes, until completely smooth. Serve with remaining croutons and season with salt and pepper.

Serves 8 to 10.

Traditional Gazpacho from Andalusia

Another great recipe from Executive Chef Santi Zabaleta (Taberna del Alabardero). Santi usually serves this soup in a small glass, not in a big bowl. The recipe is prepared the day or night before serving.

12 Roma tomatoes, diced
1/4 cucumber, peeled, seeded and diced
1/2 green pepper, diced
2 slices stale white bread, diced (crusts on)
1 or 2 garlic cloves, coarsely chopped
1 cup olive oil
1 tablespoon sherry vinegar
salt to taste

Garnish:
tomato, diced in small pieces
green pepper, diced in small pieces
cucumber, diced in small pieces
stale white bread, diced into small pieces

Combine all the ingredients in a medium-size bowl and let soak overnight in the refrigerator.
Once ingredients have soaked, puree the mixture in a blender and strain.
Place soup in the refrigerator for 2 hours. Serve soup cold.
Serves 4 or 5.

For garnish, place small diced tomatoes, green peppers, cucumber, and white bread into separate bowls, place on table and allow guests to garnish soup themselves.

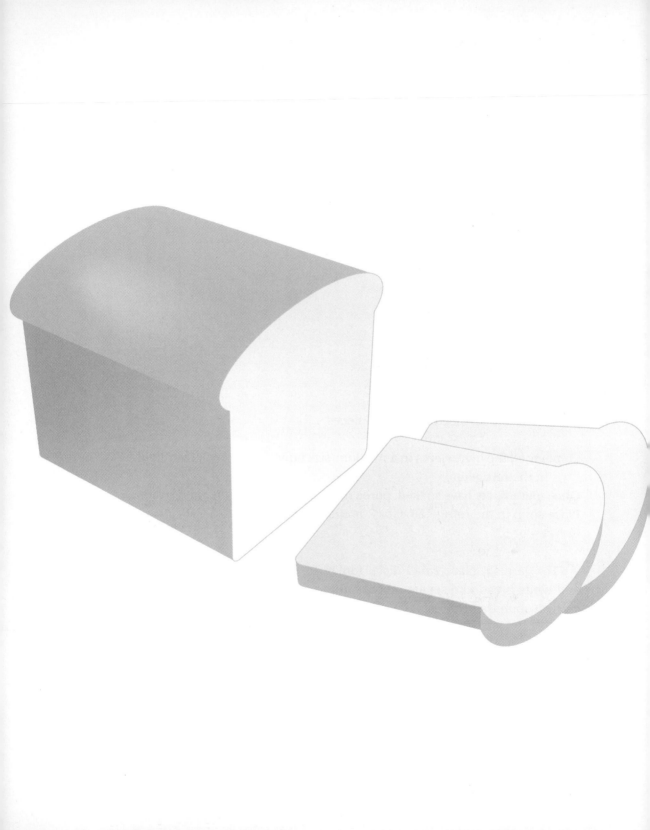

Bread as a Container

"The likely history of the pudding can be illuminated by looking back at medieval sops and at the medieval practice of using a hollowed-out loaf as the container for a sweet dish."

—*The Oxford Companion to Food*, Alan Davidson

Although the original idea behind this book was to feature recipes using leftover bread, I could not bring myself to leave out the many uses for fresh bread as containers (though there are a number of recipes in this section, including the Bruschetta recipes that use day old bread). There are so many interesting, flavorful, and unusual recipes where the bread itself serves as a base, a container, or is rolled with a variety of fillings inside. The recipes in this chapter should help you think about creating your own variations; for example, a large "Bread Croustade," which can be filled with anything from your favorite tuna or egg salad, to eggs scrambled with your favorite meats or vegetables.

Asparagus Rollups

What can be better than asparagus paired with a smooth "snappy" cheese mixture.

20 slices very soft fresh white bread with crusts removed
8 ounces cream cheese, softened to room temperature
4 ounces bleu cheese, crumbled
1 large egg
dash of Tabasco sauce
dash of Worcestershire sauce
1 (14.5-ounce) can asparagus spears, well drained
1/2 cup melted butter or margarine

Flatten the bread out by rolling each slice two or three times across with a rolling pin.
In a small bowl, combine the cheeses, egg, Tabasco, and Worcestershire sauces.
Spread this mixture evenly on each slice of bread. Place one asparagus spear on each slice of bread and roll up like a jelly roll (or log).
If the spears are longer than the slices of bread, trim off the "overhang" and use 3 or 4 such extra pieces to fill one slice of bread.
Dip each piece of the rolled-up bread in the melted butter, and slice into thirds.
If not serving right away, rollups can be frozen at this point and reheated using the regular baking directions below.
Preheat oven to 425°F. Place the rollups on an ungreased cookie sheet.
Bake for about 15 minutes or until golden. Serve hot.
Makes 5 dozen.

Bread Croustade

Preheat oven to 325°F.

Cut the top off (leaving the remaining section about 2 & 1/2-inches high) a large unsliced loaf of fresh white or other grain bread that is 1 or 2 days old.

Carefully remove the crusts and the sharp edges from each corner.

Hollow out the loaf, leaving the walls about 3/4-inch thick.

Brush the inside and outside of the bread with melted butter (clarified is best) and bake on a jelly-roll pan for 20 to 25 minutes or until croustade is golden brown.

Fill with your favorite filling, slice, and serve, or freeze empty for future use.

Brie en Croute

This is a very elegant hors d'oeuvres made with homemade brioche dough. The brioche recipe can be used to prepare a number of other recipes in this book, including French toast. This recipe is from Mark Ramsdell, the director and head instructor for L'Academie de Cuisine's professional Pastry Arts Program. I met Mark when I taught at L'Academie and later took a fabulous bread class from him. He studied under and worked at the White House with Roland Mesiner, the executive pastry chef at the White House. Ramsdell is the founder of the award-winning Pastry Design Studio, which specializes in large show cakes. It is one of Washington, DC's top ten pastry shops, and he also started Dining In, the DC area's first gourmet meal delivery service. In his "previous life," Ramsdell taught urban policy analysis and design in architecture school!

1 2-pound brie, room temperature
1 recipe brioche*
1 large egg mixed with 1 teaspoon water (egg wash)

Roll a 1-inch recipe of brioche—after its second rising—3/8 to 1/2-inch thick.

Cut two circular pieces of dough. The first piece should be large enough to cover the top of the brie and wrap over its sides. The second piece, which can be slightly thinner, should only be as big as the brie's diameter.

Brush the egg wash over the larger piece of brioche. Center the brie on the brioche.

Brush more of the egg wash over the brie and wrap the brioche around the sides and top edge of the brie. Do not pull the dough, but make it as smooth as possible.

Pinch the edges of the dough into the brie.

Brush egg wash on the second circle of brioche. Turn it over and cover the bottom of the brie. Pinch dough together.

Turn right side up, place on a sheet pan and let rise.

Preheat oven to 375°F. Bake about 30 minutes.

Serves about 16.

*Brioche

For en croute applications, the butter in a brioche recipe can be reduced to 5 ounces.

1 tablespoon yeast
1/4 cup warm water
1 pound all-purpose flour
2 ounces sugar (4 tablespoons)
1 & 1/2 teaspoon salt
5 large eggs
8-ounces butter, room temperature, cut in small pieces.

Egg wash: 1 large egg mixed with 1 teaspoon water

Proof the yeast. In a small bowl, add the yeast to 1/4 cup tepid water (best if water is about 105°F—no higher than 115°F). Mixture should appear bubbly and foamy as the yeast comes out of its "dormant" state (if this does not happen, yeast is dead and cannot be used).

Combine flour, salt, and sugar in a large mixing bowl.

Add proofed yeast to flour mixture and stir together at low speed with paddle beater of your mixer.

When dough is stiff, add eggs gradually. It should take about 5 minutes to add the eggs to the flour mixture.

Switch to a dough hook on your mixer and increase the speed of mixer. Mix brioche for about 15 minutes. When brioche dough is elastic, add butter steadily. Mix 5 minutes to incorporate.

Place dough in large bowl and cover with plastic wrap. Allow dough to rise at a warm temperature (88°F–90°F) until doubled in size, about 1 hour.

Knock down dough until it is its original size. Be sure to get all of the air out. Place dough in a plastic bag. Allow enough space in the bag for the dough to double in size. Place dough in the refrigerator (overnight) or the freezer and let rise.

Remove brioche dough from refrigerator, knock down. If frozen, defrost the dough overnight in the refrigerator.

After removing from refrigerator (after second rise) and knocking down, shape as desired. Be sure to flour work surface and use well-greased molds. Molds should only be filled halfway.

Allow dough to rise until doubled in size before baking.

Preheat oven to 375°F.

Egg wash twice. Large pieces should have slits clipped in them (with scissors) after rising to prevent cracking when baked.

Bake. Baking time varies with size of piece. Small loaves take 25 to 30 minutes, large loaves take 35 to 40 minutes. Smaller pieces take 15 to 20 minutes. Remove brioche from pans and cool on its side or on its top. Let brioche cool completely before serving or it will be soggy. *Makes about 5 (1/2 pound loaves).*

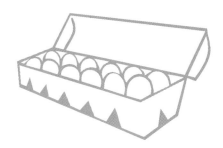

Brie in the Hole

Be prepared to hand out recipes when you serve an elegant Brie in the Hole at your next party. Make a few, each one with a different topping . . . ummm good!

5-inch wheel of Brie
1 to 2 tablespoons Dijon or fruit-flavored mustard
1/4 cup slivered almonds
1 round loaf of fresh sourdough or flavored (like olive or sun-dried tomato) bread (bread must be bigger than the Brie in diameter)

Preheat oven to 350°F. Place Brie on a baking sheet.

Cut a circle of rind from the top of the Brie leaving a l-inch border.

Spread the mustard smoothly over the top of the exposed cheese.

Top the mustard with the slivered almonds.

To cut the proper-size hole, place the Brie on top of the bread and cut a circle (around the bread) that is 2 inches wider than the cheese. Set the Brie aside.

Remove the circle (top of the bread) and dig out enough bread chunks so the cheese fits evenly into the hole, with the top of the Brie even with the top of the bread.

Cut or tear the chunks of bread and place on a serving dish.

Place the Brie in the oven and bake for 25 minutes or until Brie is soft and runny.

Let guests spread the Brie on the bread, also tearing pieces from the loaf. Crackers and party breads are also good to use.

Serves 8.

Variations: Serve Brie in the Hole with warm roasted garlic to spread on the bread before the Brie. Alternative toppings can be brown sugar and pecans or raspberries and/or raspberry syrup.

Ripe cheeses should be used as quickly as possible. Brie and Camembert should be bought just before using, leaving them out of the refrigerator an hour or two before serving. Natural cheese should be stored tightly in the original wrapping or foil.

Bruschetta Two Ways

Bread is taken very seriously in Italy. More than a mere culinary staple, bread is the cornerstone of the Italian culture, which takes deep pride in simply transforming the gifts of nature. Bread, in Italy, is even used to express the pleasant mannerisms of people. Someone with a good character, for example, would be "good . . . like bread." A big-hearted person would be "warm . . . like bread." If someone were flexible, they would be "soft . . . like bread." The list of Italian bread metaphors is endless.

These are two of my friend Amy Riolo's favorite ways to serve bruschetta, which are usually served with a variety of toppings, and are moist enough to spread easily and seep into the bread.

The first topping is an artichoke puree, which she used to enjoy when living in Rome. It was a typical antipasto served at one of her favorite pizzerias. Luckily, it is healthy and easy to make. The second topping has only two ingredients—cream cheese and roasted red peppers. Use the best quality olive oil possible. Note that the recipes call for day old bread.

Artichoke Puree

1 (4-ounce) can artichoke hearts, drained and rinsed
2 tablespoons extra-virgin olive oil
juice of 1 lemon
1/4 cup Romano cheese
salt
freshly ground pepper
2 loaves crusty, day-old Italian bread
1/4 cup extra-virgin olive oil

Place the ingredients for puree into the food processor and process until a smooth puree is formed (less than 1 minute). Taste the puree. Adjust the seasoning if necessary. Set aside.
Preheat oven to broil.
Place the bread under the broiler. Toast for 3 to 5 minutes until golden.
Remove bread from the oven and turn bread over.

Return to broiler and toast for another 3 minutes, or until golden on the
    other side.

Remove from the oven.

Slather a thick layer of the puree on each slice of bread.

Serve warm.

Serves 4. to 6.

Roasted Red Pepper Puree

8-ounce container of cream cheese
1 large roasted red pepper (from a jar), drained
freshly ground pepper
2 loaves crusty, day-old Italian bread
1/4 cup extra-virgin olive oil

Place the cream cheese, red pepper, and pepper into the food processor
    and process until a smooth puree is formed (less than 1 minute).
    Taste the purees. Adjust the seasoning if necessary. Set aside.

With a large serrated knife, slice the bread into 1/4-inch slices on the
    diagonal.

Lay the bread slices evenly on cookie sheets.

Brush both sides with extra-virgin olive oil.

Preheat oven to broil.

Place the bread under the broiler. Toast for 3 to 5 minutes until golden.

Remove bread from the oven and turn bread over.

Return to broiler and toast for another 3 minutes, or until golden on the
    other side.

Remove from the oven.

Slather a thick layer of the puree on each slice of bread.

Serve warm.

Serves 4 to 6.

Cheese Fingers

These zippy "fingers" will appeal to anyone who loves bleu cheese. This is another recipe that can be made ahead, frozen, and reheated without compromising taste.

loaf of fresh white bread with crusts removed
1 pound cheddar cheese in thin slices
1/2 pound processed bleu cheese (suitable for spreading)
2 cups grated Parmesan cheese
2 cups mayonnaise

Preheat oven to 350°F.

Place one slice of cheddar cheese on each slice of bread. Top with another slice of bread, then spread it with blue cheese.

Place another slice of bread on top of the blue cheese, making 3 slices of bread and two cheese fillings.

Spread all sides of the bread with mayonnaise and dip all sides in the Parmesan cheese.

Cut "sandwiches" into "fingers" (cutting bread into 4 equal strips)—squares or triangles—and secure with toothpicks.

Place bread on a baking sheet lined with parchment paper or on a non-stick baking pan.

Bake until golden brown, when the cheese has melted but not burned.

Each "set" of bread makes 4 fingers.

Creamy Artichoke Croustades

Make lots of the croustades ahead and freeze them until needed. Almost any filling can be used and croustades can be made in any size muffin tins, from tiny to large. The bigger size croustades can be used for entrees or to hold individual portions of vegetables. This is a rich but easy filling.

24 slices thin fresh sandwich bread, crusts removed
1 (14-ounce) can artichoke hearts, packed in water, drained well, minced
1 cup mayonnaise
1 tablespoon Dijon mustard
1 teaspoon Worcestershire
2 tablespoons grated Parmesan cheese
freshly ground pepper
salt
garnish: paprika

Preheat oven to 375°F. Using a rolling pin, roll out bread until very thin and cut circles about 2 & 3/4 inches with a round cutter (if using mini muffin tins). Larger circles will be needed for larger pans.

Press each slice into a 1 & 3/4-inch diameter cup of a mini muffin pan. Press gently with your fingers so they fit snugly.

Bake 5 to 10 minutes until lightly browned. Do not over bake. Remove from pans, place on a cookie sheet, and set aside.

Raise oven to 400°F. Squeeze out any excess moisture from artichokes and place in a large bowl. Add the mayonnaise, mustard, Worcestershire, and cheese. Mix well and stir in salt and pepper to taste.

Divide mixture among croustades and sprinkle lightly with paprika.

Bake 10 to 15 minutes, allow croustades to cool slightly and serve. May be frozen when cooled.

Makes 24.

Eggs in a Basket

Reminiscent of one of the earliest uses of stale bread as an edible serving container, this is a clever way to serve hard cooked eggs for brunch or a light supper. To round out the meal, add a spinach or citrus salad and a fruity white wine.

1/3 cup mayonnaise
2 tablespoons milk
2 tablespoons chopped chives
1/2 teaspoon dry mustard
1/4 teaspoon salt
1/8 teaspoon pepper
1 large round loaf fresh Italian bread, unsliced
5-ounce jar processed cheese spread
1/4 cup softened butter
6 hard cooked eggs, coarsely chopped
1 cup cherry tomatoes, halved
1 green pepper, coarsely chopped

In small bowl, combine mayonnaise, milk, chives, and seasonings. Refrigerate 1 hour to let flavors blend. With sharp knife, cut a circle around bread 1 inch from edge. Lift off top and scoop out bread, leaving a 1 inch shell. (Both the scooped out bread and top can be frozen for other uses.)

Place shell on cookie sheet. Combine processed cheese with butter and spread evenly over inside of shell. Bake at 400°F 10 minutes, or until cheese filling is bubbly.

Combine eggs, tomatoes, and green pepper with mayonnaise mixture and spoon into bread basket.

To serve, cut in thick wedges.
Serves 4 to 6.

 Egg yolks will stay centered if stored broad end up.

Eggs in a Hole

2 slices of good quality stale bread, white, whole wheat, or challah
2 tablespoons butter
1 tablespoon canola oil
2 large eggs
2 tablespoons grated Swiss, Gruyere, or your favorite cheese
dash Tabasco
salt
freshly ground pepper
minced fresh basil, oregano, parsley (optional)

Make a 1 & 1/2- to 2-inch hole in the center of each slice of bread.
In a small skillet over medium heat, heat the butter and oil until hot.
Add the bread slices and cook for about 2 minutes on each side to coat
    with butter/oil mixture and lightly toast the bread.
Lower the heat to medium and carefully crack an egg into each hole.
Cook for about 2 to 3 minutes to set eggs.
In a small bowl, combine the cheese and Tabasco, mixing well.
Using a metal spatula, carefully flip the toasts and sprinkle tops with grated
    cheese, and salt and pepper to taste.
Continue cooking until eggs are cooked the way you like them and the
    cheese is melted (about 2 minutes for runny yolks).
Top with chopped herbs if desired, and serve.
Serves 2.

Fabulous Hot Jarlsberg
and Onion Dip in a Bread Bowl

Hot and hearty, this is a classy way to serve a favorite dip. Any thick creamy soup can be served in the same way. A favorite company dish of my friend Paula Jacobson.

1 round loaf fresh sourdough or pumpernickel hollowed out
2 cups shredded Jarlsberg cheese
1 medium onion, quartered and thinly sliced
1 cup mayonnaise, regular or light
dash of fresh nutmeg

Preheat oven to 350°F.

Cut a hole about 5 inches in diameter in the top of the bread. Reserve crusty part and cube for dipping. Place bread on an ovenproof baking dish.

Scoop out most of the soft inside portion of the loaf and save for dipping into the cheese, or save for stuffing or bread crumbs.

In a medium-size bowl, combine all cheese, onions, mayonnaise, and nutmeg, mixing well.

Place cheese mixture in the bread and bake for 25 to 30 minutes or until cheese is melted and golden. Stir cheese mixture (while in bread) once or twice.

Serve with vegetables, bread cubes, French bread, or crackers. Dip can be made early in the day and baked later.

Serves 12 or more.

Glorious Garlic Loaf

This recipe uses the loaf as a "basket" or container and uses the chunks of bread (that are removed when making the basket) for filler. This marvelous appetizer can be made ahead or frozen and can be a vegetarian main course when served with a salad.

1 pound loaf fresh French bread
1/2 cup butter or margarine
6 garlic cloves, crushed
2 tablespoons sesame seeds
1 & 1/2 cups sour cream
1/4 cup grated Parmesan cheese
8 ounces Monterey Jack cheese, cubed
1/3 cup chopped fresh parsley
2 teaspoons lemon pepper
1 (14-ounce) can artichoke hearts, drained
1 cup cheddar cheese, shredded
6-ounce can pitted black olives (optional)

Preheat oven to 350°F. Slice the bread in half lengthwise.
Place bread on foil-covered baking sheets.
Tear out large chunks of the soft insides of the bread, leaving the crusts intact.
In a large skillet, melt the butter and stir in the garlic and sesame seeds, stirring and cooking for a minute.
Stir in the bread chunks and cook until the bread is golden and butter has been absorbed. Remove from heat.
In a large bowl, combine the sour cream, Parmesan, Monterey Jack cheese, parsley, and lemon pepper. Stir in drained artichokes and toasted bread mixture, mixing well.
Spoon mixture into the halved bread crust shells and sprinkle with cheddar cheese.
Bake for 30 minutes.
Drain the olives. Remove the bread from the oven and arrange olives around edges if desired. Slice and serve hot.
Serves 8.

Wash and store parsley in a tightly covered jar in the refrigerator. This will keep it fresh for a long time.

Mock Cheesecakes

I have been making and teaching these for thirty-eight years, and they are still requested by students who already know how to make them (they just want to eat them). They are very addictive.

2 (22 ounces each) loaves of fresh sliced white bread, with crusts removed
1 pound cream cheese, softened to room temperature
2 to 3 tablespoons milk
1 & 1/2 tablespoons almond extract
1 cup or more melted butter or margarine
1/2 cup sugar mixed with 1 tablespoon (or more, to taste) cinnamon

Preheat oven to 350°F.

With a rolling pin, roll each piece of bread, separately, back and forth a few times to flatten it.

In a small bowl, with an electric mixer at medium speed, beat the cream cheese with enough milk to make it easy to spread. Beat in almond extract.

Spread the cream cheese lavishly on each slice of bread.

Roll the bread up tightly the long way, so it looks like a cigarette.

Place melted butter in a pie pan. Place sugar/cinnamon mixture in another pie pan.

Dip each piece of rolled bread into the melted butter. Run your fingers down the sides of the roll to remove any excess butter. Then roll in the sugar/cinnamon mixture.

Cut each roll into 3 pieces and place on a lightly greased or sprayed cookie sheet.

Bake for 5 minutes. Cool slightly and eat.

If you are freezing them, let them cool completely and place into freezer bags.

To reheat frozen cheesecakes, preheat oven to 400°F and bake frozen on a cookie sheet for about 5 to 8 minutes or until hot.

Makes about 8 dozen.

Mushroom Croustades

As a young bride, this was the most elegant appetizer I knew how to make. Creamy and rich, they are worth the time it takes to prepare the filling. They can be made ahead, refrigerated (or frozen), and reheated.

canola spray
24 slices soft, thinly sliced fresh white bread, crusts removed
1/4 cup butter or margarine
3 tablespoons finely chopped shallots
1/2 pound fresh mushrooms, wiped and chopped fine
2 tablespoons flour
1 cup heavy cream, or cream substitute
salt
freshly ground pepper
pinch of cayenne pepper
1 tablespoon finely chopped fresh parsley
1 & 1/2 tablespoons finely chopped fresh chives
1/2 teaspoon lemon juice
3 tablespoons grated Parmesan cheese
additional butter or margarine for topping

Preheat oven to 400°F. Spray the insides of 24 3-inch muffin tins (or 36 or more mini muffin tins) with the canola spray.

Cut each slice of bread with a 3-inch round cookie cutter (or smaller for mini tins), and carefully press into the greased tins, molding them in the tins to form little cups.

Bake for 10 minutes or until lightly browned. Remove croustades from oven and their tins, and set aside for filling (or cool and freeze until needed).

Reduce oven to 350°F.

In a large skillet, melt the butter and sauté the shallots over medium heat, stirring for 3 minutes. Stir in the mushrooms and cook, stirring, for about 15 minutes or until moisture has evaporated.

Remove skillet from the heat, whisk in the flour, blending well, then whisk in the cream and return the skillet to the heat.

Bring the mixture to a boil, stirring constantly, and as the mixture thickens, turn the heat to low and cook another minute or two.

Remove the pan from the heat, stir in the seasonings, herbs, and lemon juice. Place the mixture in a bowl to cool—the entire recipe may be made ahead to this point.

About 15 minutes before serving, fill the croustades with the mushroom filling, sprinkle the tops with Parmesan cheese, and dot the tops with the additional butter.

Place the croustades on an ungreased cookie sheet and bake for 10 minutes. Serve immediately.

Makes about 24.

Onion Rounds

Two versions, each quick, easy, and elegant. Your guests will keep coming back for more.

2/3 cup mayonnaise
1/3 to 1/2 cup freshly grated Parmesan cheese
1 small onion, finely chopped
2 to 3 loaves fresh miniature rye or pumpernickel bread
paprika

Preheat the oven to broil.
Combine the mayonnaise, cheese, and onion and spread mixture on top of the bread.
Sprinkle top of each with paprika. Place slices on a lightly greased cookie sheet and broil 6 inches from the heat until bubbly. Watch them carefully as it only takes about a minute.
Serve hot. These rounds can be assembled in advance and broiled just before serving.
Makes 2 & 1/2 to 3 dozen.

Version 2

1 large loaf (22 ounces) fresh white bread, crusts removed
2 medium red onions, diced
1/2 cup mayonnaise
1/4 cup grated Parmesan cheese
1/4 cup grated Romano cheese
1/4 cup chopped parsley

Preheat oven to 350°F.
Using a biscuit cutter, cut each slice into a circle 2 to 3 inches in diameter.
Sprinkle a small amount of the diced onion on each circle of bread.
In a small bowl, combine the mayonnaise, Parmesan, and Romano

cheeses; spread enough of this mixture on each circle to cover the onions.

Sprinkle parsley on top.

Place the rounds on a lightly greased cookie sheet and bake for 10 minutes or until bubbly. Serve hot. Baked rounds may be frozen and reheated on a cookie sheet at 350°F for 15 minutes or until heated through.

Makes 2 & 1/2 to 3 dozen.

Summer Pudding

Summer pudding is a traditional English-Irish pudding that is made by lining a mold (I use a 2-quart charlotte mold or soufflé dish) with bread and a filling made of a variety of fresh berries (or frozen). The spongy, moist pudding is made twenty-four hours before serving and weighed down on top so the fruit and bread can amalgamate into a solid dessert that can be unmolded onto a serving platter. Note that fresh bread is used in this particular dessert. Summer Pudding can be made without the wine syrup, just the juice from the cooked fruit and sugar.

22-ounce loaf of thin-sliced fresh white (or challah) bread, crusts removed—if possible, use a fresh bakery-made bread
3 cups red wine, such as a Merlot
1 cup sugar
a cinnamon stick
8 cups of fresh berries (a combination of raspberry, blueberry, blackberry, or sliced strawberries can be used or defrosted frozen berries)
2 (1/4 ounce each) packets gelatin
garnish: fresh berries (optional)

Cut bread slices to fit lengthwise around the sides of the mold (remove crusts) and across the bottom, plus enough for two additional layers inside the mold and across the top.

In a 4- or 5-quart non-reactive pan, bring the wine, sugar, and cinnamon to a boil, stirring to mix well and dissolve sugar.

Reduce heat to simmer and carefully add fruit. Stir gently, simmer fruit for 3 minutes, then drain fruit and place in a bowl, saving the syrup. Chill the fruit in the refrigerator.

Line the mold with plastic wrap with 4 inches hanging over at least 2 of the sides.

Carefully dip each piece of bread needed with syrup and line mold along the sides (overlapping the pieces slightly) and bottom, cutting and adding additional pieces to make them fit snugly if necessary.

Fill the bread casing with 1/3 of the fruit, top with dipped bread that fits snugly.

Top with 1/3 of the fruit, then dipped bread, and then the remaining fruit and dipped bread.

Take remaining syrup and combine 1 cup of it with the gelatin, stirring well to dissolve.

Then warm the syrup without the gelatin and stir in the cup of gelatin syrup, mixing well.

Pour about a cup of the syrup over the top of the Summer Pudding, a little more may be used if needed.

Bring the side pieces of plastic wrap over the top, adding more wrap if needed.

Weigh down top with pie weights, rice in a plastic bag, or cans.

Refrigerate overnight.

To serve, remove weights and unfold plastic wrap, pulling the top pieces to the side as you unmold the pudding onto a serving platter.

Serve with fresh whipped cream or ice cream if desired.

Serves 8.

Veal Marengo en Croustade

This hardy, elegant, breath-taking dish is sure to please any guest!

4 tablespoons olive oil, divided
2 pounds veal cut into 1/2-inch cubes
salt
freshly ground pepper
2 & 1/2 tablespoons all-purpose flour
2 tablespoons tomato paste
1 large garlic clove, crushed
1 cup dry white wine
10.5-ounce can chicken broth

Bouquet Garni:
tie into a cheese cloth: 1 celery stalk with leaves, chopped, 1 teaspoon thyme, and 1
    small bay leaf
1 pound mushroom caps, cleaned and cut in half if large
20 small pearl onions, fresh (peeled), canned, or frozen drained
1 pint small cherry tomatoes, washed and stems removed
2 tablespoons fresh parsley, minced (for garnish)

Croustades:
2 (1 pound each) loaves fresh French or Italian bread or 6 small individual rounds of
    bread
1/2 pound butter or margarine

Heat 2 tablespoons oil in a large pot and sauté the veal cubes, in batches (being care-
    ful not to crowd them or they will stew). Turn, and brown on all sides. Remove
    from pot and place in a bowl.
After all the meat has cooked, return it to the pan along with the juices.
Stir in the salt, pepper, and flour, stirring to coat meat well.
Add the tomato paste, garlic, wine, broth, and spices (Bouquet Garni). Stir, bring to a
    boil, reduce heat and simmer. Cover and cook for an hour.

Heat remaining 2 tablespoons of oil in a large skillet. Over medium heat, sauté the mushrooms until golden. Push them to one side and sauté onions, turning often, until a pale gold. Set aside.

To prepare croustades:

Preheat oven to 350°F.

Remove all crusts and slice each loaf crosswise into 3 equal cubes.

Cut a circle around the inside of each cube, leaving about 1/2-inch wall on all sides and bottom. With a knife, carefully remove center of cubes, or hollow out center of individual loaves of bread.

Brush all surfaces with the melted butter, place on a baking sheet and bake 15 to 20 minutes or until golden, and set aside.

When ready to serve, stir into the heated veal mixture the mushrooms, onions, and cherry tomatoes, stirring gently just to heat through (about 5 minutes).

Discard Bouquet Garni.

Place croustades on serving plate and spoon some of the veal mixture into the center, allowing some of the veal to spill over onto the plate. Sprinkle with parsley.

Serves 6.

 A pinch of salt in the frying pan will keep grease from splashing.

Savory Bread Puddings

"Puddings in all their variety and glory may thus be seen as the multiple descendants of a Roman sausage, and the Haggis, by its nature and the way it is prepared, illuminates the connection."

—*The Oxford Companion to Food*, Alan Davidson

*B*read puddings may be dressed up or down, turned sweet or savory, depending on the occasion and the meal demand. They can accent the meal either as the main course, side dish, or dessert. And to assure their versatility, bread puddings are just as delicious served hot or cold, sauced or plain.

The term "pudding," when it first appeared in the thirteenth century originally referred to intestines or guts. Because puddings (intestines) were used as containers for cooking, the finished foodstuff became a "pudding." For hundreds of years there were two categories of puddings—black puddings, made of blood, and white puddings, made of chicken, veal, or grain. Both varieties of pudding were stretched with fat, fillers, and seasonings. By the fifteenth century, pudding recipes already called for bread crumbs and fillers made from a compound of flour or meal, eggs, and milk. On occasion, dried fruits like raisins, currants, dates, and prunes also showed up. While people added raisins and dried fruits, the term "plum pudding" did not appear until the eighteenth century, when it was referenced in the *Oxford English Dictionary* in 1711.

Davidson (*Oxford English Companion to Food*) points out that pudding may be claimed as a British invention and is a characteristic dish of British cuisine. But the Portuguese and Spanish also have similar claims. Davidson concludes by saying, "Puddings in all their variety and glory may thus be seen as the multiple descendants of a Roman sausage. The Haggis by its nature and the way it is prepared, illuminates the connection."

The history of pudding is confusing since many different foods have been known by this name. Food historians tell us that bread puddings date back to early times when it was a common practice to use stale/hard bread to avoid waste, including its use as an edible serving container (medieval sops), a stuffing (forcemeat), special dishes, French toast, and thickeners. Bread crumbs and egg yolks were used to thicken sauces before flour thickeners were used in cooking. In addition, "sippets" or "tost" (toast), was used as sop-pieces to soak up liquid mixtures. The bread was first toasted, which reduced its tendency to disintegrate.

According to Kathleen Curtin, food historian at the Plimoth Plantation, in Plymouth, Massachusetts:

> It would be difficult to over emphasize the place of puddings, sweet or savory, fancy or humble in the diet of 17th century Englishmen. Puddings of all sorts were mainstays in the diet of every Englishmen. Poor Englishmen ate basic puddings (porridges) of boiled oats while the wealthy not only ate these staple dishes but also fancier puddings. There were sweet rice or oat puddings, black puddings (blood puddings), liver puddings, savory puddings, and a huge variety or bread puddings that were boiled in guts or a bag, dried, cooked like dumplings or simmered in a post as a 'hasty pudding.' A lot of these fancier puddings were made with costly ingredients and sophisticated techniques. Cooks of the time understood the chemistry of cooking, including the proportions of egg yolks which provided richness and a delicate texture to whites which strengthen and toughen. In 17th century England (and New England), sweet puddings were not considered a 'dessert' as we

know it. Instead they were eaten as part of the meal, along with the meat and other dishes. While today we tend to think of pudding as a homey comfort food that takes advantage of stale bread, for centuries these sort of sweet puddings were viewed as a more luxurious food since they used costly dried fruits and spices.

Francois Maximilien Misson, a French visitor during the late-seventeenth century, described to his French readers how the English made puddings. "They bake them in an oven, they boil them with meat, they make them fifty several ways; blessed be he that invented pudding, for it is a manna that hits the palates of all sorts of people . . . Ah, what an excellent thing is an English pudding! To come in pudding time, is as much as to say, to come in the most lucky moment in the world."

Until the beginning of the sixteenth century, puddings were boiled. By then some homes had their own small ovens built into the chimney breast. Because they did not get very hot, it was easy to slowly bake a white pudding or a cereal pottage.

The seventeenth century also brought another important change— the invention of the pudding cloth, which eliminated the need for making pudding in animal gut. Simple boiled puddings (porridges) were already an important and expected side dish for the nineteenth-century table, occasionally served as a separate course (in more formal households), and as a cheap filler in more common homes. Many puddings were flavored not by seasonings added during preparation, but by use of either a sweet or savory sauce when being served. Thus a boiled flour pudding or bread pudding, which appears somewhat blah from reading the recipe, is transformed into a rather flavorful dish by the use of a savory gravy.

By the nineteenth century, the use of intestines for puddings had virtually disappeared except for blood puddings. Even cloth pudding bags were being replaced by containers made of tin (referred to as pudding bags in a tinner's price list) or by baking the pudding in a paste (piecrust).

As the household servant class diminished in the twentieth century, more and more housewives took over the task of cooking, and many had a difficult time using the pudding cloth that their servants had traditionally used. Boiled puddings, therefore, began to be made in basins or molds, which were covered with greased paper (like waxed paper) and foil and steamed partly immersed in water. This tradition continues today.

Hints and Tips

If possible use only bakery or bakery-quality bread not packaged commercial bread.

Since most of the recipes rely on day old or stale bread, you can dry out fresh bread's natural moisture by crisping it (or cubes or crumbs) on a cookie sheet in a 200°F oven for a few minutes. Do not let brown. Or, let your bread sit out overnight in the air.

When measuring bread crumbs or cubes, do not pack them down in the measuring cup, just pile them in lightly.

In most recipes, trimming away crusts is optional. You will have a slightly denser pudding if you include them in your measurement; softer, more soufflé like if you don't include them.

It is best to assemble and refrigerate many bread puddings ahead of cooking so the custard can be absorbed, resulting in a creamier texture.

Many puddings are cooked in a water bath, which surrounds the delicate custard-base dishes with gentle heat to keep them from separating.

Use a metal or glass baking pan or a large roasting pan for the water bath.

Most bread puddings are best served warm from the oven.

If scalding milk and/or cream is called for, rinse the pot in cold water first, but don't dry it out. This will prevent the milk from scorching the bottom of the pot! Scalding is heating the milk and/or cream just below the boiling point. Tiny bubbles will appear around the edges.

2 slices bread equal 1 cup bread cubes

Bagel and Cheese Strata

Another quick and easy winner that is prepared the day or night before serving. This fabulous recipe is courtesy of *Vegetarian Times* magazine (April 2004). Besides being a fabulous brunch dish, the strata can be made lower in fat by using egg substitutes.

canola spray for greasing
7 large eggs (or 1 & 3/4 cups egg substitutes)
1/4 teaspoon salt
2 cups milk
1/2 teaspoon paprika
freshly ground pepper
4 plain bagels, halved, cut into bite-size cubes
6 ounces Monterey Jack cheese, grated, or Jack with pepper
6 ounces cheddar cheese, grated

Lightly grease a 2-quart baking dish. Beat together eggs, salt, milk, paprika, and pepper in a mixing bowl. Set aside.

Place half of bagel cubes in the baking dish.

In a medium-size bowl, mix the grated cheeses together. Sprinkle half of the cheese mixture on top of bagel cubes. Top with remaining bagel cubes and remaining cheese.

Carefully spoon the egg mixture over bagel-cheese layers, poking holes in bagels with a fork or knife to assure that egg mixture seeps in evenly. Cover dish with aluminum foil and refrigerate overnight.

Preheat oven to 350°F. Bake strata for 1 hour, or until top is golden brown.

Remove from oven, and serve hot.

Serves 6 to 8.

Basil and Pine Nut Bread Pudding

The Mediterranean flavorings of this bread pudding make it a favorite of Marie Huntington (from her book *Cooks & Company*). Marie is a well-known cooking teacher and the former owner of Cooks & Company, in Indiana.

butter for greasing
1 cup half-and-half
3/4 cup heavy cream
4 large eggs, beaten
stale French bread, crust removed, torn into pieces (to make 4 cups)
salt
freshly ground pepper
1 small onion, finely diced
1 tablespoon chopped fresh basil
1/3 cup pine nuts
1 stalk celery, finely diced

Preheat the oven to 400°F. Butter a 1-quart baking dish.
Combine half-and-half, cream, eggs, bread, salt, pepper, onion, basil, nuts, and celery in a mixing bowl and blend well. The mixture should be very creamy.
Add more half-and-half if needed.
Pour mixture into prepared baking dish and let rest at room temperature at least 2 hours.
Bake for 45 minutes. Remove from the oven and cut into squares.
Makes 6 servings.

Eggs should not be washed at home. Incorrect washing procedures could contaminate the eggshell's contents. Cracking and leaking eggs should be discarded since cracks allow bacteria to enter through the shell (even if the egg is not leaking).

Bread Pudding with Turkey, Dried Apricots, and Pecans

My friend Amy makes this all year round using ingredients found in the deli section of the supermarket. The taste is a real balance of sweet and savory.

2 stale baguettes (not crunchy, crusty long ones, but the softer crust, foot-long type)
2 tablespoons butter or margarine, divided
1 pound turkey (spiral sliced honey turkey from deli counter), cubed 1/4-inch pieces
1 cup dried apricots (from California), diced
1 cup chopped pecans
1 cup grated Parmesan (good quality) (vegetarian Parmesan is available)
6 large eggs
3 cups whole milk or milk substitute
2 teaspoons cumin
1 teaspoon salt

With serrated knife, cut bottom crust off of each baguette.
Then cut into 1/2-inch cubes. You can do this the day before to let the moisture evaporate slowly or put on a shallow pan to dry out in a 300°F oven (less than 10 minutes), and remove cubes before they get golden.
Butter a 9x13-inch casserole dish (use metal pan if you want crusty edges) with 1 tablespoon (or less) butter.
Layer bread, turkey, and apricots into dish.
Whisk eggs, milk, cumin, and salt and pour over ingredients in casserole dish.
Gently press down to make sure all bread is absorbing the egg mixture.
When time to cook,* preheat oven to 350°F.
Put pecans and remaining butter in a glass measuring cup and microwave just long enough for butter to begin to melt. Stir to coat nuts.

Sprinkle half of Parmesan, then all of nuts, and then rest of Parmesan over the top.

Bake for 45 minutes or until puffy and center doesn't jiggle.

Turn oven to broil. Broil one minute, just to brown the top a bit.

Rest 5 minutes before serving.

Serves 6 to 8.

*Amount of time for absorption can be as little as five minutes or overnight. For any amount of time over 15 minutes, keep dish covered, in refrigerator. Add 15 minutes to cooking time if chilled for longer than an hour.

How To Toast Pecans: When you toast pecans, you bring their sugar and oil to the surface, providing a more intense flavor. Preheat the oven to 325°F, place nuts on a cooking sheet in a single layer and bake for 5 minutes. Watch carefully as they will burn easily. If the recipe calls for chopped toasted pecans, always chop before toasting.

Etta's Cornbread Pudding

This is one of only two recipes in the book that suggests making your own bread. I pigged out on this when I ate at Etta's, a famous Seattle restaurant, and decided to include the whole recipe as Chef Tom Douglas gave it to me. I found it interesting that Chef Tom began making special breads just for bread pudding, in this case cornbread. If you don't want to prepare Tom's cornbread, make your own or buy a good quality one from a store.

Etta's cornbread pudding is made with a dry Jack cheese, which is nuttier and tangier than regular Jack cheese (like Vella Dry Jack from Sonoma, California), but you could use sharp cheddar instead. The flavor of the cornbread pudding would change but would be equally delicious. Douglas serves this cornbread pudding with Etta's Pit Roasted Salmon, but it would be equally delicious with other salmon recipes.

This recipe makes more cornbread than you need to make the Cornbread Pudding. You can freeze the extra cornbread for future batches of Cornbread Pudding, or, if you're like us, you can snack on it while it's warm with butter and honey.

For cornbread:
1 cup all-purpose flour
3/4 cup cornmeal
1/2 cup (1 & 1/2 ounces) grated pepper Jack cheese
1 teaspoon baking powder
1 teaspoon salt
2 large eggs
1 cup milk
3 tablespoons honey
4 tablespoons unsalted butter, melted plus a little more for buttering pan
    (for the cornbread)
1 tablespoon unsalted butter plus a little more for buttering pan (for the
    pudding)
1 cup thinly sliced onion, about 1/2 large onion
3/4 cup grated dry Jack cheese, regular Jack, or sharp cheddar
2 teaspoons chopped flat leaf parsley
1/2 teaspoon chopped fresh rosemary

1/2 teaspoon chopped fresh thyme
2 & 1/4 cups heavy cream
4 large eggs
1 teaspoon kosher salt
1/2 teaspoon freshly ground black pepper

To make the cornbread, preheat the oven to 425°F. Butter an 8x8-inch
baking dish. Combine the flour, cornmeal, cheese, baking powder,
and salt in a large bowl. In another bowl, whisk together the eggs,
milk, and honey. Add the wet ingredients to the dry ingredients, stirring until just combined. Melt 4 tablespoons of the butter and stir
into the mixture. Pour into the prepared pan and bake about 15 to
20 minutes until a toothpick comes out clean.
Cut into 1-inch cubes. You should have about 8 cups of cornbread cubes,
but you only need one third of the cornbread cubes (or 2 & 2/3 cups)
for this recipe.

To make the Cornbread Pudding, lower the oven temperature to 350°F.
Put the 2 & 2/3 cups of cornbread cubes in a buttered 8x8-inch baking
dish. Set aside.
Heat 1 tablespoon butter in a sauté pan on low heat and very slowly sauté
the onions until soft and golden brown, at least 20 minutes. Remove
from the heat and let cool.
Scatter the onions, cheese, and herbs over the cornbread cubes.
Whisk together the cream and eggs with the salt and pepper and pour
over the pan of cornbread cubes. Let sit 10 minutes so the cornbread
cubes absorb some of the custard. Bake about 40 minutes or until
set and golden. Serve warm.
Serves 6.

You can make the cornbread and store it in the freezer wrapped
tightly in plastic for a few weeks, until you are ready to make the cornbread
pudding. The onions can be caramelized a day ahead and stored in the
refrigerator. The cornbread pudding can also be baked a day in advance
and stored in the refrigerator, covered. Before serving, reheat the cornbread
pudding covered with foil in a 375°F oven until warmed through, about
35 to 40 minutes.

Equinox's Butternut Squash and Lamb Bread Pudding

Equinox, owned by Ellen and Todd Gray, is one of the top restaurants in Washington, D.C. Here, the Grays have created an oasis of sophisticated yet unpretentious seasonal cuisine, in a fabulous location, just one block from the White House.

2 tablespoons grapeseed or canola oil
1 onion, peeled and minced
2 garlic cloves, minced
1 butternut squash, peeled and diced
1/2 pound lamb stew meat, ground
salt
freshly ground pepper
4 cups dry/stale sourdough bread crumbs
4 large eggs, beaten well
1 cup milk, or non-dairy substitute
1 cup heavy cream, or non-dairy substitute
1/3 cup grated Parmesan cheese, or vegetarian substitute
dash of ground nutmeg (optional)
dash of Tabasco (optional)

Preheat oven to 400°F. Grease a 9x13-inch baking pan.

In a large sauté pan, heat oil to high-medium temperature. Add onion, garlic, and squash, mix well and cook, stirring, for 5 minutes.

Add lamb, salt and pepper to taste, and cook, stirring to mix well, another 5 minutes.

Remove pan from the heat, pour off any remaining grease and set aside to cool.

In a large bowl, combine cooled lamb mixture with bread, beaten eggs, milk, cream, and cheese. Add nutmeg and/or Tabasco if desired.

Mix well and spoon into prepared pan.

Bake for 30 minutes or until custard is set. Remove from oven and let sit 5 to 10 minutes. Cut into serving pieces, and serve.

Serves 8.

To avoid crying when chopping onions, refrigerate the onions for an hour, make sure you use a sharp knife, slice the root area last (since there are a greater number of enzymes in that area), and light a candle right next to the area where you are chopping. The rising "smoke" will carry away a lot of the fumes that cause crying.

Green Chili Bread Pudding

These zippy individual bread puddings are similar to my recipe for cheese squares that I fondly call "Texas Fudge." In this recipe from Flo Braker, French bread and chili powder are added to make this as piquant or as hot as you like. Flo is the author of *The Simple Art of Perfect Baking*, *Sweet Miniatures*. She is currently working on another baking book to be published in 2008. Flo has been the baker columnist for the *San Francisco Chronicle* since 1989 and is a past president of the International Association of Culinary Professionals (IACP).

butter for greasing
5 large eggs
1 cup whole milk
2/3 cup heavy cream
1 teaspoon or more chili powder
1/4 teaspoon salt
1/4 teaspoon ground cumin
1/4 teaspoon dried oregano
3/4 cup (2.5 ounces) loosely packed, coarsely shredded sharp cheddar cheese
1/3 cup (1.5 ounces) loosely packed coarsely shredded Monterey Jack cheese
3 tablespoons canned diced (chopped) green chilies
6 &1/2 cups trimmed and cubed (1/2-inch pieces) stale French or Italian bread

Adjust rack to lower third of oven. Preheat oven to 350°F. Place a piece of foil on the rack.
Generously butter a 12-cup standard (scant 1/2 cup capacity) muffin tin.
In a large bowl, whisk the eggs, milk, and cream to blend thoroughly.
Mix in the chili powder, salt, cumin, and oregano, then mix in the cheeses and chilies.
Add the bread and mix thoroughly.
Divide the mixture evenly among the muffin tin cups.

Bake 25 to 30 minutes, or until a knife blade inserted into the centers comes out clean. Cool 5 to 10 minutes. Slide a knife blade around puddings to loosen them; lift out of molds with a small metal spatula. Serve warm or at room temperature.
Serves 12.

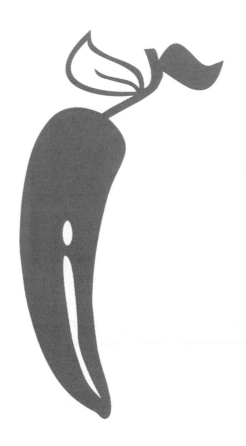 Red spices keep best when stored in the refrigerator.

Individual Garlic Bread Puddings

Often referred to as the "stinking rose," Allium Sativum is its name and garlic's popularity spans the globe. These individual bread puddings are like popovers: heavy, dense, and delicious. If you love garlic, this recipe is for you.

canola spray for greasing
10 to 12 garlic cloves, minced
3/4 teaspoon kosher salt
1 cup milk
1 cup heavy cream
2 large whole eggs
2 large egg yolks
freshly ground pepper
3 tablespoons minced fresh parsley leaves (optional)
2 & 1/2 cups stale croissant cubes (1/2-inch cubes) (about 4 or 5 croissants) or challah cubes

Butter or grease a 12 cup (1/3 cup each) muffin tin, being sure to do the sides as well as the bottoms.

Crush the garlic and salt together in a mortar and pestle to make a paste, or use the flat side of a large chopping knife. (You can also chop them together in a mini-food processor, then crush with a knife blade to make paste.)

In a medium-size saucepan, over medium high heat, scald the milk and cream with the garlic paste.

Remove pan from heat and let the mixture stand for 15 minutes.

Place a sieve over a bowl and strain the milk mixture through the sieve. Discard the garlic.

In a large bowl, whisk together the whole eggs and the yolks. Slowly add the milk whisking constantly. Add the pepper and parsley if using, and mix well.

Divide the bread cubes among the muffin cups and spoon the custard mixture over them as evenly as possible. Gently press bread down into custard with your fingers so all the cubes get soaked. Let the bread puddings stand for 10 minutes.

The puddings may be prepared up to this point 8 hours in advance and kept covered and chilled.

Preheat the oven to 350°F.

Bake the puddings for 30 to 35 minutes or until golden brown and puffed. Remove from the oven and let cool for 5 to 10 minutes (they will sink as they cool).

Run a metal spatula or thin knife around the side of each pudding and remove from tin carefully with a fork. Serve while warm.

Serves 12.

Variation: Cooked, chopped, well-drained cooled spinach (about 10 ounces) and a dash of nutmeg can also be added to the custard. You will need more muffin tins though.

 When selecting garlic, choose bulbs that are hard with a thin, dry, paper-like outer skin (usually white and tinged with pink or lavender). Avoid those that appear yellowed or are soft to the touch—they are past their prime. The rule of thumb with garlic is: the larger the clove, the more subtle the flavor, therefore elephant garlic should not be used in place of regular bulb garlic in cooking.

Lunch for Two with Cheese, Tomato, and Peppers

Company stopping by for lunch? This quick and easy bread pudding is foolproof and filling. Serve with a salad. From Norene Gilletz's *The Food Processor Bible*.

canola spray for greasing
2 slices stale whole-wheat bread, quartered
1/2 cup mozzarella cheese (low-fat is fine)
1 medium or large tomato, quartered
1/2 green bell pepper, cut into chunks
2 large eggs (or 1/2 cup egg substitute)
1 cup milk (skim or soy will work)
salt
freshly ground pepper
1/4 teaspoon dried basil
1/4 teaspoon dried oregano

Preheat oven to 375°F. Lightly grease 2 soup bowls.

In a food processor with metal blade, process the bread and the cheese for 5 or 6 seconds. Place in a bowl and set aside.

In a food processor, quickly pulse the tomato and bell pepper with quick on and off pulses.

Return the bread and cheese mixture to the processor along with the eggs, milk, and seasoning. Fill each bowl to within one inch from the top.

Bake for 25 to 30 minutes, or until puffed and golden.

Serves 2.

Marbled Rye Bread Pudding with Cheddar and Chives

This hearty dish, courtesy of my friend Amy Peck Abraham, looks gorgeous on the buffet table, can be used for brunch or dinner, and can be made ahead, frozen, and reheated. Just serve with a salad. Ideal for cold days when you want to warm your insides. Amy used to be a Senate staffer. Now, since she moved to St. Louis, she calls herself a "Professional Dilettante" and writes for a restaurant magazine, tutors adults in English as a second language, sings with the St. Louis Harmony chorus, and teaches at Dierberg's School of Cooking.

approximately one tablespoon butter or margarine for greasing
3 tablespoons butter or margarine, softened (more if needed)
1 pound loaf stale marbled rye bread, sliced (like Pepperidge Farm's)
1 pound any flavor sausage, bulk style, cooked (remove casing) and drained
    (vegetarian substitutes are okay)
4 cups shredded cheddar cheese, divided evenly
1 small (3/4 ounce or 1/2 cup) container fresh chives, chopped fine
6 large eggs plus 3 large yolks
3 cups 2% milk (or non-dairy substitute)
1 tablespoons Dijon mustard
1 teaspoon salt
1/2 teaspoon freshly ground pepper
dash of Tabasco (optional)

Let bread slices sit out (to expose them to air) for a few hours, or place on a shallow pan to dry out in a 300°F oven for less than 10 minutes, removing before they get golden.

Grease a 9x13-inch casserole dish (use metal if you want crusty edges) with 1 tablespoon or less of butter.

Spread remaining butter on bread slices and cut slices in half.

Layer bread, sausage, half the cheese, and chives in rows, placing the slices in at an angle so that casserole looks like toppled dominoes.

Whisk eggs, yolks, milk, mustard, salt, pepper, and, if desired, Tabasco.

Pour over all in the casserole dish.

Gently push bread down to make sure all bread is absorbing the egg
    mixture.
When time to cook,* preheat oven to 350°F.
Sprinkle remaining cheese on top.
Bake for 45 minutes or until puffy and center doesn't jiggle. Rest 10 min-
    utes before serving.
Serves 12.

*Amount of time for absorption can be as little as 5 minutes or over-
night. For any amount of time over 15 minutes, keep dish, covered, in
refrigerator. Add 15 minutes to cooking time if chilled longer than an
hour.

Mediterranean Strata

Strata is a savory bread pudding, and I find them great to use as a brunch dish.

1 tablespoon extra-virgin olive oil
1/2 small onion, diced
1 small zucchini, sliced
1-ounce package dried wild mushrooms, rehydrated, and chopped
1 clove garlic, minced
4 large eggs
1 cup milk
2 tablespoons julienned fresh basil
1/4 cup shredded Italian cheese blend
salt
freshly ground pepper
1/4 cup roasted red bell pepper strips
3 cups stale olive bread cubes

Preheat oven to 350°F. Coat an 8x8-inch pan with cooking spray.

Heat the oil in a medium-size skillet over medium heat. Sauté the onion, zucchini, and mushrooms for 5 to 6 minutes or until softened. Add garlic and sauté about 30 seconds more, then remove pan from heat.

In a medium-size bowl, whisk eggs, milk, basil, cheese, and salt and pepper to taste together.

Layer half of the veggies in the bottom of the prepared baking pan, and top with half the bread cubes. Repeat the layers and top with the bell pepper strips.

Pour the egg mixture over the bread and vegetables; press gently down on the bread cubes to make sure all are soaked with the egg mixture. Bake about 45 minutes, until liquid is set and top is golden.

Serves 4.

Olive and Brie Appetizer Bread Pudding

This classy pairing of your favorite assortment of olives and luxurious Brie is a first-rate first course or luncheon or brunch fare. The recipe comes from a wonderful book called *New Fangled, Old Fashioned Bread Puddings* by Linda Hegeman and Barbara Hayford. Linda and Barbara suggest making this spread in either 4 1-cup or eight 1/2-cup soufflé/ramekins. Being too lazy to grease all these dishes, I made it in a Pyrex 9x5-inch loaf pan and baked it for 65 minutes. Serve hot or cold.

butter for greasing

4 (1/2-inch each, about 1 ounce) slices of stale French bread (if bread is too hard it will not absorb the custard)

4 ounces Brie cheese, rind removed, at room temperature

4 ounces cream cheese, at room temperature

3 large eggs

1 cup milk

1 tablespoon chopped fresh oregano, or 1 teaspoon dried oregano

1 cup coarsely chopped pitted olives, of mixed varieties

Preheat oven to 300°F. Generously butter 4 1-cup or eight 1/2-cup soufflé/ramekins.

Tear the bread into small pieces and divide equally among prepared ramekins.

In a large bowl, with an electric mixer set on low speed, cream both cheeses until blended.

Add eggs, one at a time, beating until thoroughly blended after each addition.

Gradually add milk; continue beating until well mixed. Stir in oregano and olives.

Pour custard mixture evenly over bread.

Set ramekins in an ovenproof pan just large enough to hold them snugly and add enough hot water to the pan to come halfway up the sides of ramekins.

Bake for 50 minutes or until custard is set (knife inserted off center comes out clean) and tops are golden brown.

Remove from water bath onto a wire rack and cool for 20 minutes.

Serve in the ramekins (warm or at room temperature) with your favorite crisp cracker.

Let unused portions come to room temperature, cover, and refrigerate.

Serves 4 as a light luncheon serving, or 8 appetizer servings.

Pesto Bread Pudding Soufflé

This bread pudding looks like a soufflé but the sun-dried tomatoes add the pizzazz of a pizza. Serve it as an entrée with a salad or as a side dish. This is another wonderful recipe that will win you raves (from Linda Hegman and Barbara Hayford's book *New Fangled, Old Fashioned Bread Puddings*). This recipe can be started the day before baking.

butter for greasing
about 6 slices, stale, firm-textured white bread
about 4 ounces prepared or homemade basil pesto
5 large eggs
1 cup whole milk
3/4 cup heavy or whipping cream
1 garlic clove, minced
1/4 teaspoon salt
1/4 cup sun-dried tomatoes, packed in oil, patted dry, coarsely chopped
1 & 1/2 cups (about 6 ounces) lightly packed grated provolone cheese
      (easier to grate while frozen)
1/2 cup grated Parmesan cheese

Generously butter a 1.5-quart soufflé or deep-sided baking dish.
Spread pesto on one side of the bread slices and cut bread slices into 1/2-inch cubes. You will need a scant 5 cups. Set aside.
In a large bowl, using an electric mixer set on medium speed, beat together the eggs, milk, cream, garlic, and salt until well mixed.
Place half the bread cubes in the prepared dish. Top with half of the tomatoes, half the provolone, and half of the Parmesan. Repeat layering.
Slowly pour custard mixture over bread and cheese.
Gently press down with your hands or the back of a spoon, so that the bread absorbs the liquid.
Cover with plastic wrap and refrigerate several hours or overnight.
Preheat oven to 325°F.
Remove plastic wrap and cover pudding with aluminum foil. Place a large piece of foil under the dish in the oven and bake for 1 hour.

Uncover and continue to bake for an additional 10 minutes, or until cus-
tard is set (knife inserted 1 inch from the center comes out clean),
pudding is puffed, and top is golden brown.
Remove from oven onto a wire rack and let cool for 10 minutes.
Spoon onto serving plates. Serve warm or at room temperature.
Let unused portions come to room temperature, cover, and refrigerate.
Serves 6.

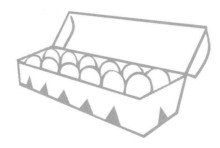A bulb or head of garlic is really a group of many cloves encased
in a skin. To quickly and easily peel garlic, lay the clove on a flat surface
and using the flat side of a large knife, press down firmly until the papery
skin breaks away and you can peel it off.

Quiche without a Crust

The quiche (or Swiss cheese tart) is a popular fixture of French cuisine, and one that is quite rich as well. By eliminating the crust, you not only save time, but you also conserve calories.

4 slices stale bread
3 tablespoons melted butter or margarine
8 large eggs
1 & 1/2 cups cream (or milk, regular or low-fat)
1/2 teaspoon salt
1/8 teaspoon nutmeg
2 cups (8 ounces) grated Swiss cheese
1 cup julienned vegetarian meat (or favorite vegetarian substitute)

Place bread slices on cookie sheet and bake in 250°F oven just until dried out; increase oven temperature to 350°F.
Cut bread into cubes and toss with melted butter in bottom of 10-inch pie pan.
Spread evenly over bottom.
In large bowl, beat eggs with milk, salt, and nutmeg.
Fold in cheese and "meat" and pour over bread cubes.
Bake 35 to 40 minutes or until knife inserted in center comes out clean.
Let cool on wire rack 10 minutes before cutting into wedges.
Serves 4 to 6.

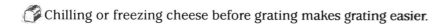Chilling or freezing cheese before grating makes grating easier.

Savory Bread Pudding with Basil and Cheddar Cheese

Susan Belsinger's passion for basil led her to grow nearly one hundred varieties, which she discusses in her book *Basil: An Herb Lover's Guide,* co-authored with herb grower Thomas DeBaggio. She finds smelling and tasting basil to be a sensory experience and encourages cultivating and cooking with her favorite herb.

Both eggs and cheese are great with basil. In this recipe, the roasted red pepper is added to contrast the richness of this dish. It makes a savory, filling main course when served with a vegetable or fruit salad; it would also make a good brunch entree.

Being lazy and not a great lover of red peppers, I used about 1/4 cup of chopped roasted red peppers from a jar.

butter for greasing
5 tablespoons unsalted butter, divided
8 slices stale French bread or a good country-style wheat bread (bread with substantial character), sliced about 5/8-inch thick
1 small onion, diced (about 3/4 cup)
1 small red bell pepper, roasted, peeled, seeded, and diced into 3/4-inch pieces
3 cups milk
2 large cloves garlic, minced
6 extra-large eggs
1 teaspoon salt
freshly ground pepper
1 cup packed, chopped basil leaves
1 & 1/2 cups grated sharp cheddar cheese

Preheat oven to 375°F. Butter a 2-quart oval gratin or casserole dish.

Butter the bread, using 2 tablespoons of the butter. Cut the bread into cubes, just under an inch in size. Set aside.

Melt the remaining 3 tablespoons of the butter in a sauté pan, add the onion and sauté over medium-low heat for 5 minutes, stirring occasionally.

Add the bell pepper, stir, and remove from heat.

In a non-reactive saucepan, heat the milk to scalding. Remove from heat and stir in the garlic.

Beat the eggs in a bowl with the salt and generously season with pepper.

Add about 1/2 cup of the hot milk to the eggs and whisk well.

Add the onions and peppers to the eggs, stir, and pour the egg-and-vegetable mixture into the remaining milk; stir well.

Add the basil and stir to combine.

Place half of the bread in the prepared baking dish and cover evenly with half of the cheese.

Pour half of the egg and vegetable mixture over the bread and cheese.

Repeat with the remaining bread, then the egg and vegetables; arrange the bread and vegetables with a fork if necessary.

Cover the casserole with the remaining cheese.

Have ready enough boiling water to come 1 to 1 & 1/2 inches up the sides of a pan large enough to hold the 2-quart baking dish.

Carefully place the pan with boiling water in the oven and place the baking dish in the pan.

Bake for 30 minutes, until golden brown. Remove the baking dish from the oven and the pan of hot water.

Let stand for 5 minutes and serve hot.

Serves 6.

When stored in a cool, dry place, fresh garlic heads will keep for several months at a time, but place them where air can circulate freely. If possible, do not place them in the refrigerator, as this will attract damaging moisture to them.

Seafood Strata

If desired, seafood can be combined with the sea bass in this recipe to give a different taste and texture.

canola spray for greasing
10 to 12 slices stale white bread, crusts removed
1 bunch fresh asparagus, cooked and cooled
2 cups diced or chopped cooked sea bass (or other fish or seafood)
12 ounces (3 cups) grated Swiss cheese or Monterey Jack
6 large eggs (or 1 & 1/2 cups egg substitute), at room temperature
3 & 1/4 cups milk or half-and-half
1/4 cup dry sherry or dry vermouth
1/4 cup minced scallions
freshly ground pepper to taste
1 teaspoon Dijon mustard
minced parsley (optional)
cherry tomatoes (optional)
olives (optional)

Lightly spray a 9x13-inch baking pan and cover the bottom of the pan with bread.

Place a layer of cooked asparagus over the bread, followed by a layer of fish, then cheese.

Repeat the layers, starting with the bread and ending with the bread until all the bread, asparagus, seafood, and cheese are used.

In a large bowl, lightly whisk together the eggs, milk, wine, scallions, pepper, and mustard.

Spoon the egg mixture over the top of the prepared layers then cover and refrigerate for a minimum of 6 hours, or overnight if possible.

Preheat oven to 325°F. Bake the strata, uncovered, for about one hour. Remove from the oven and let strata rest for 10 minutes before serving. Garnish with minced parsley, cherry tomatoes, or olives if desired. Serve hot.

Serves 8 to 10.

Sourdough Bread Pudding with Salmon, Asparagus, and Jarlsberg

My friend Amy says, "This is very yummy!" The combination of ingredients makes this an elegant comfort food and a lovely buffet dish.

1 loaf stale sourdough (softer crust, round type)
1 tablespoon butter
1/2 pound Jarlsberg cheese, thinly sliced
1/2 pound smoked salmon, crumbled
1 pound asparagus, blanched then cut on diagonal into 1-inch pieces
3/4-ounce container fresh dill, finely chopped
4 large eggs and 2 large egg whites
3 cups half-and-half
2 teaspoons salt

Using a serrated knife, cut loaf in half. Tear out bread from crust in small pieces. You can do this the day before to let the moisture evaporate slowly, or put on shallow pan to dry out in a 300°F oven, less than 10 minutes, remove before they get golden.

Butter a 9x13-inch casserole dish (use metal if you want crusty edges).

Layer bread, half the Jarlsberg, salmon, asparagus, and dill into dish.

Whisk eggs, egg whites, half-and-half, and salt, mixing well.

Pour over everything in the casserole dish and gently press down, to make sure all bread is absorbing the egg mixture.

When time to cook,* preheat oven to 350°F.

Place remaining slices of Jarlsberg on top with gaps between the slices.

Bake 45 minutes or until puffy and center doesn't jiggle.

Turn oven to broil, and broil 1 minute just to brown the top a bit. Rest 5 minutes before serving.

Serves 12.

*Amount of time for absorption can be as little as 5 minutes to overnight. For any amount of time over 15 minutes, keep dish, covered, in refrigerator. Add 15 minutes to cooking time if chilled for longer than an hour.

 Hard cheeses keep the best (Swiss, cheddar, and Edam) unopened. Sliced cheeses stay fresh slightly less than 3 to 4 weeks.

Southwestern-Style Chicken Strata

A strata is a custardy egg casserole and is a meal-in-a-dish that is best when assembled the night before. It will puff up and turn golden brown like a soufflé and takes very little work to prepare. Substitutions for a kosher version are listed.

In this recipe you can substitute jalapeno cornbread for the sourdough bread, and hot pepper cheese for the Monterey Jack cheese. If you use those two ingredients, you can eliminate the diced green chilies. This recipe is from my friend and fellow food writer Ginnie Manuel.

canola spray for greasing
10 slices stale sourdough bread (1 pound loaf cut into 1/2-inch slices)
3 cups (12 ounces) shredded Monterey Jack cheese (or vegetarian cheese)
2 cups bottled mild red salsa (I love it with mango salsa with peach, drained
	slightly), more if desired
2 to 2 & 1/2 cups diced cooked chicken (can substitute vegetarian)
15-ounce can black beans, rinsed and drained
6 large eggs, well beaten
2 & 1/4 cups milk (non-dairy creamer)
4-ounce can diced green chilies, drained (optional)
salt
freshly ground pepper

Several hours or the day before serving, line bottom of spray-coated
	9x13-inch metal baking dish with half the bread slices.
Sprinkle with half the cheese, half of the salsa, half of the chicken, and
	half the beans.
Repeat layers with remaining bread, cheese, salsa, chicken, and beans.
In a small bowl, beat eggs with milk, chilies if using, and seasonings.
Pour over bread mixture, cover and refrigerate 8 hours or overnight.
Preheat oven to 350°F. Bake uncovered until edges are browned and center is set, about 50 to 55 minutes.
Cool 15 minutes before cutting into rectangles.
Serves 8.

Tenderize chicken by rubbing the inside and outside with lemon juice before cooking.

Swiss Tuna Bake

This delicious but easy dish can be assembled the night before and baked an hour before your guests arrive. This can also be made as a low-fat dish. The recipe is from Norene Gilletz's *The Food Processor Bible*.

canola spray for greasing
3 green onions, cut into chunks
1/4 cup fresh dill
1 cup fresh mushrooms, cleaned
2 (7 ounces each) cans tuna, drained and flaked
salt
1 cup grated Parmesan cheese, divided
2 cups grated Swiss or Gruyere cheese (8 ounces), divided
6 slices stale white or whole-wheat bread (or half of each)
4 large eggs (or 2 eggs plus 4 egg whites)
1/2 teaspoon dry mustard
1 teaspoon Worcestershire sauce
3 or 4 drops hot sauce
2 cups milk (regular or low-fat)

Place the onions, dill, and mushrooms in the food processor and pulse until finely chopped.

Place in a large mixing bowl and add tuna, salt, and half the Parmesan cheese. Add half of the grated Swiss cheese to the tuna mixture.

Add the remaining grated Swiss cheese to the remaining Parmesan cheese and set aside.

Grease an 11x7-inch glass baking dish. Trim the bread and place in the baking dish.

Spread tuna mixture over the bread.

In the processor, pulse together the eggs, mustard, Worcestershire, and hot sauce for 2 to 3 seconds.

Add the milk through the feed tube while machine is running.

Immediately pour over tuna mixture. Top with reserved cheeses. Cover and refrigerate for at least 2 hours or overnight.

Preheat oven to 350°F. Bake covered for 30 minutes, then uncover, and bake another 30 minutes. Let sit 5 minutes before cutting and serving.

Serves 6.

Tomato Pudding

Similar to Bess Truman's, this is a nice, no-fuss, no-mess side dish. This version uses tomato sauce; others use homemade tomato puree and more brown sugar. This recipe is a favorite of Susie Marshall, a fellow member of THIS (The Hospitality and Information Service).

1 & 1/3 cups tomato sauce
1/4 cup boiling water
2/3 cup brown sugar
1/2 cup melted butter
7 slices stale white bread with crusts removed

Preheat oven to 375°F.
Place tomato sauce in a 1-quart pan and add the water and sugar.
Mix well and bring to a boil.
Reduce heat to simmer and continue stirring and cooking another 5 minutes.
Place 6 slices bread in a 9x13-inch baking dish. Cut the 7th piece to fill in any gaps.
Pour the butter over the bread.
Pour the tomato mixture over all and bake for 30 minutes.
Serves 6 to 8.

Wild Mushroom Bread Pudding

The French bistro tradition is interpreted with contemporary American flair at Barrington Country Bistro, in Barrington, Illinois (www.barringtonbistro.com). This hearty, aromatic mushroom bread pudding is a seasonal special, regularly featured as an accompaniment to entrées of duck or game, or as an anchor for a vegetarian plate. Chef Luis Quiroz enjoys varying this specialty with exotic seasonal mushrooms and premium breads, like his buttery homemade brioche. The recipe below is simple to follow and will produce delicious results for the beginner and the gourmet cook alike. But, the Bistro invites you to bring it your own contemporary flair—just add your favorite ingredients (like cloves of roasted garlic or pieces of Brie) or alter the seasonings or spices to complement its partners on the plate.

butter for greasing
3 or more tablespoons olive oil
6 ounces shiitake mushrooms, stemmed, caps thickly sliced
6 ounces oyster mushrooms, thickly sliced
6 ounces crimini mushrooms, thickly sliced
2 portobello mushrooms, stems and gills removed, caps thickly sliced
4 teaspoons chopped garlic
1 tablespoon chopped fresh basil
1 tablespoon chopped fresh parsley
1 teaspoon dried rubbed sage
1 teaspoon dried thyme
5 large eggs
2 cups whipping cream
1 cup milk (do not use low-fat or nonfat)
1/4 cup plus 2 tablespoons freshly grated Parmesan cheese
3/4 teaspoon salt
1/2 teaspoon ground pepper
6 cups 1-inch cubes crustless stale French bread (about 6 ounces)

Preheat oven to 350°F. Lightly butter 8x8x2-inch glass baking dish.
Heat oil in heavy large pot over medium-high heat. Add all mushrooms,

garlic, basil, parsley, sage, and thyme and sauté, stirring occasionally, until mushrooms are tender and brown, about 15 minutes.

Remove pot from heat. Season mixture to taste with salt and pepper.

Whisk eggs, cream, milk, 1/4 cup Parmesan, salt, and pepper in large bowl to blend.

Add bread cubes; toss to coat. Let stand 15 minutes.

Stir in mushroom mixture. Transfer to prepared dish.

Sprinkle 2 tablespoons cheese over top. Bake until pudding is brown and puffed and set in center, about 1 hour. Serve warm.

Serves 6 as side dish.

Mushrooms are fresh when the gills do not show and the cap is close to the stem.

Wine and Cheese Omelet Bread Pudding for a Crowd

It's hard to find easy but delicious do-ahead brunch dishes, or a great after midnight dish to "ring in" the New Year. This make-ahead dish produces two large pans and can be frozen for future use! This is from my friend Marilyn Bagel.

canola spray for greasing
1 large loaf stale French or Italian bread, broken into small pieces
6 tablespoons unsalted butter, melted
1 pound Swiss cheese, shredded
1 pound Monterey Jack cheese, shredded
16 large eggs
3 cups skim milk
1 cup dry white wine
4 large green onions, minced
1 tablespoon Dijon mustard
freshly ground pepper
1/2 teaspoon red pepper
dash of hot sauce (optional)
1 cup regular or low-fat sour cream
2/3 to 1 cup grated Parmesan cheese

Spray two shallow 9x13-inch baking dishes.
Spread the bread over the bottoms of the pans and drizzle with butter.
Sprinkle with the Swiss and Jack cheeses.
Beat the eggs, milk, wine, green onion, mustard, pepper, red pepper, and hot sauce (if desired) until foamy. Pour over the cheeses.
Cover dishes with foil and refrigerate overnight or up to 24 hours.
Preheat oven to 325°F.
Remove dishes from the refrigerator about 30 minutes before baking and let come to room temperature.
Bake casseroles, covered, until set—about 1 hour.
Uncover casseroles and spread with sour cream and sprinkle with Parmesan cheese.
Bake uncovered until crusty and lightly browned—about 10 minutes.
Each pan serves at least 12.

Sweet Bread Puddings

- Apple and Cheese Bread Pudding 135
- Apple Bread Pudding 136
- Banana Bread Pudding with Easy Caramel Sauce 137
- Bangkok Joe's Ginger Bread Pudding 139
- Blackberry Bread Pudding with Wild Turkey
  (Whiskey) Sauce 141
- Bread and Butter (Nursery) Pudding 143
- Brioche Bread Pudding with Italian Orange Pastry Cream 144
- Capirotada (Mexican Bread Pudding) 146
- Challah Bread Pudding with Carrot Crème Anglaise 147
- Chocolate Cherry Croissant Bread Pudding 149
- Chocolate-Chocolate Bread Pudding with White
  Chocolate Sauce 150
- Chocolate Fig Bread Pudding with Spirited Sauce 152
- Chocolate Marmalade Croissant Bread Pudding 154
- Christmas Bread Pudding 155
- Dixie's Bread Pudding 157
- Dominic's Pumpkin Bread Pudding with Caramel Sauce 158
- Inn at Little Washington's Custard Bread Pudding with
  Two Sauces 160
- Lemon Meringue Bread Pudding 162
- New Mexico Bread Pudding 164
- Om 'Ali (Egyptian Bread and Butter Pudding) 166
- Orange-Spice Rhubarb Betty 168
- Peach Melba Bread Pudding with Raspberry Sauce 170

"It is safe to assume that from the very distant past cooks have sometimes turned stale bread into a sweet pudding. If only by soaking it in milk, sweetening it by one means or another, and baking the result. The addition of some fat, preferably in the form of butter, and something like currants is all that is needed to move this frugal dish into the category of treats."

—The Oxford Companion to Food, Alan Davidson

I was born with a sweet tooth and a severe craving for chocolate, into the wrong family. My mother's idea of a satisfying dessert was a vanilla wafer or a piece of un-iced sponge cake; while I, on the other hand, if presented with an iced cake, would devour the icing and throw away the cake. My problem was solved when, at the age of eight, my mom taught me how to bake. I started with brownies and rapidly progressed to chocolate cakes, fudge, and a variety of chocolate cookies. Of course, some time passed before I discovered the joys of bread puddings, but when I did, they became one of my favorite comfort foods—and I am not alone!

If baking bread connotes home and hearth, family ties, and comfort foods, then bread puddings take that sense of nostalgia one step further. They are just as delicious served hot or cold, sauced or plain. Even better, they may be dressed up or down, depending on what the occasion and the meal demands, and turned sweet or savory, and used as a preamble, main course, or dessert. They offer a wonderful way to take the edge off chilly evenings or to use up leftover bread. In Jewish households that must use up or throw out all leavened bread before the Passover holidays, they can be especially attractive.

Alan Davidson points out in *The Oxford Companion to Food* that cooks in medieval times used a hollowed-out loaf as the container for a sweet dish, which later evolved as bread pudding.

Bread puddings were originally developed as sturdy foods to feed invalids. According to author "Miss Leslie," in *Directions for Cookery in Its Various Branches* (1849), American cooks took bread puddings a step further by dressing them up in a fanciful variety of ways—in a lavish use of butter, rich milk, wine and brandy, rose water and lemon peel. These desserts were exceedingly popular as fashionable hostesses iced them with meringues and served them with a variety of sauces.

Later, in Britain, a pudding came to be narrowly defined as "the principal or normal kind of sweet course at the end of a meal."

From the eighteen century and into Victorian times, the British pudding was unsurpassed. According to Delia Smith (in her book *Delia Smith's Complete Cooking Course*), "George I (Pudding George—hence the nursery rhyme about Georgy-Porgy) was particularly partial to the boiled variety. Later Prince Albert became a champion of our puddings . . . and the royal chefs were very busy creating new temptations for the royal palate: Queen's Pudding, Windsor Pudding, Empress Pudding, and Albert Pudding."

Bread puddings were popular in America in colonial times, and recipes can be found in a number of eighteenth- and nineteenth-century cookbooks. At first these were usually rich and interestingly flavored with fruits, jams, spices, meringue, and other delicacies, but plain puddings remained popular. Eventually the rich and interestingly flavored were simplified into the bland "nursery" milk pudding of succeeding centuries.

As the nineteenth century progressed, puddings increasingly became a starch-thickened, sweet-milk-based foodstuff, much more akin to people's concept of pudding today. By the late nineteenth century, puddings had taken their place in the dessert category, along with another traditional filling side dish—pies. Summer puddings, which made use of fresh fruits and were prepared by baking or steaming, can also be traced back to this time period. They were identified with healthy living and as a good food for the sick.

Bread puddings have been among the favorite recipes of many of the presidents of the United States. *The First Ladies Cook Book* (Parents Magazine Press, 1965) tells about each president and the dishes they liked to serve in the White House. Bread puddings made from sponge cake or Naples biscuits were a popular dessert served by the Washingtons. John and Abigail Adams liked to serve Beggar's Pudding made with stale bread, rose water, ground ginger, and nutmeg. Thomas Jefferson's (the "grand gourmand") favorite was Wyeth's English Plum Pudding prepared with a quart of grated bread crumbs, a quart of beef suet, citron, candied orange peel, candied lemon peel, raisins, and a cup of brandy, which he served with a "hard sauce" flavored with rum. John Quincy Adams had a favorite Chicken Croquette recipe that he liked to serve to company and a Baked Codfish Pie, both prepared with stale grated bread or bread crumbs. Millard Fillmore served Roast Capons stuffed with forcemeat made with bread crumbs, and Andrew Johnson served a Stuffed Eggplant, Spanish Style, which called for seasoned bread crumbs in the filling. Woodrow Wilson liked Old Virginia Cornbread Stuffing for his roast turkey, and Bess Truman used bread crumbs in her Meat Loaf, while Mamie Eisenhower loved to serve Tomato Pudding.

For a time, bread puddings were considered an old-fashioned dessert, but no more. Amy Whorf in her article, "It's Puddyng Time!" (*Country Living*, April 1991) says of bread pudding, "Tried and true's now 'hot' and new."

From cookbooks dating from 1796 to the late twentieth century, the continuing popularity of bread pudding affirms its place among classic American dishes. In his book, *Classic Home Desserts* (Houghton Mifflin), Richard Sax states: "Bread puddings are something you remember being fed while visiting your grandmother's . . . then came the 1980's and old fashioned standbys like bread pudding exploded onto restaurant menus on several continents and in various incarnations."

According to cooking schools, teachers, chefs, restaurant owners, and some newspaper articles, diet trends (high carb, low carb) and fads are constantly changing, but people still want their desserts! Even if it is just a small piece of something sweet; no matter what diet they follow, when friends come over or when they entertain, desserts are still a must.

The traditional bread pudding recipes in *Upper Crusts* include a few simple ingredients that cooks usually have on hand: the requisite stale bread, milk or cream, eggs, sugar, vanilla, possibly chocolate, and a variety of optional spices, nuts, or fruits. This combination will serve you well whenever you are looking for a quick, simple, and economical comfort-food dessert. But like many other time-honored favorites (rice pudding, pumpkin pie, macaroni and cheese), bread pudding has received an enormous number of new treatments by adventurous cooks. Such diverse ingredients as chocolate, bourbon, cheese, apples, coconut, and mangoes have been called into service to create desserts that rise above the ordinary.

Upper Crusts provides many new ways to break with traditional bread puddings in a tantalizing fashion. In addition, there are no intimidating techniques or hard-to-find ingredients, and they are a pleasure to prepare. Many of these delights will undoubtedly become "new traditions." Times have changed and these recipes, with a few exceptions, can be assembled in less than 30 minutes. Most can be made ahead or frozen and don't create a mess during preparation, all of which will make them appealing to busy, contemporary cooks.

Even my mother—she of the vanilla wafers and un-iced sponge cake—would find these recipes impossible to resist. Enjoy!

Apple and Cheese Bread Pudding

The combination of fresh apples and grated cheddar cheese makes this contemporary version truly unique.

1 cup brown sugar
1/2 cup water
canola spray for greasing
6 slices firm bread, toasted and cubed
1/2 cup golden raisins
1 peeled, thinly sliced baking apple
1/4 cup melted butter or margarine
2 large eggs
1 & 1/2 cups milk
1 teaspoon cinnamon
1/4 teaspoon nutmeg
1/2 cup grated cheddar cheese
nonfat vanilla frozen yogurt or your favorite yogurt or ice cream flavor, for serving

In small saucepan, combine sugar and water and boil over medium-high heat until thick and syrupy, about 5 minutes; set aside.
Spray a 9-inch-square baking pan and layer half the bread cubes, syrup, raisins, and apples; repeat with remaining bread, syrup, raisins, and apples.
In medium bowl, combine butter, eggs, milk, cinnamon, and nutmeg.
Pour over bread mixture.
Preheat oven to 350°F. Bake 35 minutes.
Sprinkle with cheese and bake 5 minutes longer, or until melted.
Cool on wire rack before cutting into squares. Serve with scoops of frozen yogurt.
Serves 6 to 8.

Apple Bread Pudding

This quick, easy bread pudding made with fresh chopped apples or applesauce (if you don't want to bother chopping your own) is from an Eagle Brand recipe brochure.

butter for greasing pan
3 large eggs
14-ounce can Eagle Brand Sweetened Condensed Milk
23-ounce jar chunky applesauce or 2 & 1/2 to 3 cups chopped apples
1 & 3/4 cups hot water
1/4 cup melted butter
1 teaspoon ground cinnamon
1 teaspoon vanilla
4 cups bread cubes cut from a loaf of stale French bread
1/2 cup golden raisins

Preheat oven to 350°F. Butter a 9x13-inch baking pan.
In a large bowl, beat eggs then add milk, applesauce or apples, water, melted butter, cinnamon, and vanilla and beat to mix well.
Stir in bread cubes and raisins, press gently to moisten completely on all sides.
Turn into prepared baking dish and bake for 60 minutes or until a knife inserted in the center comes out clean.
Cool and serve warm with ice cream, whipped topping, or a dessert sauce.
Cover and refrigerate leftovers.
Serves 6 to 8.

Banana Bread Pudding with Easy Caramel Sauce

This recipe comes from the 2003 Cookbook of the Year, *Cooking Class: A Chef's Step-by-Step Guide to Stress-Free Dinner Parties that Are Simply Elegant!* by Carol Dearth. Based on seasonal menus for dinner parties, the book is a complete how-to-do-it guide to dinner parties. She constantly seeks to share her knowledge and enthusiasm with her readers and students at her own school, RainCity Cooking School, in Bellevue, Washington, or other cooking schools around the country. For a variation: add or substitute shredded coconut or your favorite chopped nuts with or in place of the chocolate chips.

2 tablespoons butter, plus a little for the dishes
2 large eggs
1 cup whole milk or half-and-half
1 teaspoon almond extract (or vanilla if you don't have almond)
dash freshly grated nutmeg
6 cups stale challah (crust on or off), cut in 3/4-inch cubes
1 banana
1/4 cup brown sugar
2 teaspoons Amaretto
1/4 cup chocolate chips (optional)
1 tablespoon slivered almonds
2 teaspoons sugar, for topping
4 to 6 tablespoons Easy Caramel Sauce (*see recipe below*) or purchased
     caramel sauce
12 thin banana slices

Preheat oven to 350°F. Generously butter insides of a 1/2-quart soufflé
     dish or 8x8-inch baking pan.
In a bowl combine eggs, milk, almond extract and nutmeg.
In large bowl, pour egg mixture over bread cubes, stir to mix well. Set
     aside for 15 minutes, stirring occasionally.
Meanwhile, quarter banana lengthwise, then cut into 3/4-inch pieces.

Melt butter in medium skillet over medium-high heat. Add banana pieces and brown sugar, cook until sugar is melted and bubbly, about a minute or two.

Remove pan from heat, stir in liqueur, and let cool.

Combine banana and egg mixtures, stir in chocolate chips.

Spoon into prepared ramekins. The recipe can be prepared to this point 4 to 5 hours in advance. Cover and refrigerate until ready to cook.

Sprinkle top of puddings with slivered almonds, then sugar.

Bake in preheated oven 20 to 25 minutes. Top should be golden brown and crunchy. Serve warm, drizzled with caramel sauce and garnished with banana slices.

Serves 4 but can be doubled.

Easy Caramel Sauce

This is by far the easiest caramel sauce I have ever made. It is rich and smooth textured with a beautiful golden color.

14-ounce can sweetened condensed milk

Pour the milk into a 5- to 6-cup ovenproof dish with a lid. Cover tightly.

Place the dish in a larger ovenproof dish. Pour water in the outer dish to a depth of 1 & 1/2 inches.

Bake at 350°F for 1 & 1/2 hours, stirring occasionally.

Whisk to smooth consistency, if necessary. Cool. If desired, stir in 1 teaspoon vanilla extract or rum.

Store cooled caramel in a "squeezer" bottle in the refrigerator. Bring to room temperature to soften before use. The caramel will keep for 2 months.

To keep bananas fresh for longer periods, wrap each one in its peel in aluminum foil, and place it in the vegetable bin of your refrigerator. Remove the banana from the refrigerator for a few minutes before eating. Bananas stored in this manner will keep for up to 3 weeks.

Bangkok Joe's Ginger Bread Pudding

At Bangkok Joe's in Washington, D.C., chef/owner Aulie Bunyarataphan presents a menu of traditional Thai dishes that are updated with a modern American twist. With this home-style *Ginger Bread Pudding,* she does the reverse, incorporating an Asian influence into traditional American bread pudding.

"Custard desserts are very popular in Thailand. After experimenting with a variety of Asian herbs in milk-based desserts, I've found that ginger works the best and creates a wonderful flavor," says Aulie. The rich custard pudding in this recipe is simmered with fresh ginger root before being combined with cubes of French bread. Served warm and cut in a square, Aulie adds dark raisins and ginger candy for crunch, and as a finale, tops it off with powdered sugar, whipped cream made with dark rum, and toasted almonds.

4 cups coconut milk
4 cups heavy cream
1 head (large) fresh ginger root, chopped fine and crushed/smashed with
     a mortar and pestle
12 to 16 large eggs
2 cups sugar
1/2 cup ginger candy, sliced
1/2 cup dark raisins
2 stale loaves French baguette, cubed

Preheat oven to 325°F degrees. Combine coconut milk, heavy cream, and
     ginger-root, and heat to just below boiling for 15 minutes. Blend the
     eggs with the sugar until smooth. Temper the eggs with the hot milk
     cream mixture by slowly pouring and continuously whisking the
     mixtures together, then strain.
Pour the custard over cubed bread in a 9x13-inch baking pan and let it sit
     for about 10 minutes.
Sprinkle ginger candy and raisins on top and bake in a water bath until
     set and firm, about 1 hour. Let it cool and cut into 12 squares. Serve
     warm.
Serves 12.

Variation:

Fold in prepared whipped cream with Myers's dark rum. Add a dollop of whipped cream to each square and sprinkle with powdered sugar and toasted almonds.

Ginger is best when you can peel it with your fingernail—if it is this fresh, you do not have to peel it for use in the recipe. Look for ginger with smooth skin (wrinkles indicate that the root is dry and past its prime). It should have a fresh, spicy fragrance. Fresh unpeeled ginger root, tightly wrapped, can be refrigerated for up to 3 weeks and frozen for up to 6 months. To use frozen ginger, slice off a piece of the unthawed root and return the rest to the freezer.

Blackberry Bread and Butter Pudding with Wild Turkey (Whiskey) Sauce

8-ounce loaf stale French bread cut into 1 & 1/2-inch cubes
3 large eggs
3 large egg yolks
1 & 3/4 cups sugar
2 tablespoons vanilla
1 teaspoon ground cinnamon
1 teaspoon freshly grated nutmeg
1/4 pound unsalted butter, softened
2 cups milk
2 cups heavy cream
2 quarts fresh blackberries (frozen have too much liquid)

Wild Turkey (Whiskey) Sauce

2 cups milk
2 cups heavy cream
1/2 vanilla bean
2 & 1/2 cups sugar, divided
12 egg yolks
salt to taste
Wild Turkey Whiskey to taste
1/2 to 3/4 cup whipped heavy cream (optional)

Preheat the oven to 350°F. Toast the bread cubes in the oven until golden
  brown. Remove from the oven and transfer to a non-greased 13x9x2-
  inch baking pan.
Leave the oven on 350°F.
With a heavy duty mixer (not a hand mixer) beat the whole eggs and the
  yolks until frothy.
Slowly beat in the sugar, vanilla, cinnamon, and nutmeg and blend well.
Add the softened butter, and mix well.
Add the milk and cream and beat until mixed well.

Spread the blackberries evenly over the toasted bread cubes.

Pour the custard mixture over the berries and bread and press gently until they are thoroughly soaked.

Bake until golden brown, about 30 to 40 minutes. While it is baking the pudding should rise 2 to 3 times its original height but it will settle to only slightly higher than its original size. After baking, cool pudding slightly and serve with Wild Turkey Sauce if desired.

Prepare sauce while pudding is baking. In a 2-to-3 quart pot over medium heat, heat the milk, cream, vanilla bean, and half of the sugar just to boiling.

In a stainless steel bowl, mix the yolks with the rest of the sugar and the salt.

Pour 1/4 cup of the hot mixture into the eggs, beating (whisking) constantly.

Then beat in another 1/4 cup of the hot mixture, and add the eggs back to the remaining hot milk, whisking well.

Cook egg/milk mixture over low heat, stirring or whisking constantly. Continue cooking until sauce is thick enough to coat a wooden spoon.

Place a fine sieve or colander over a bowl and strain the mixture.

Fill a larger bowl with ice. Place the bowl with the strained mixture into a larger bowl filled with ice and let the sauce cool.

When mixture is cool, fold in the whiskey and the whipped cream.

Serve with the bread pudding.

Serves 8 to 10.

Bread and Butter (Nursery) Pudding

This recipe used to be known as Nursery Pudding and has been popular in Britain for over two hundred years. This version is a favorite of author/food writer Clarissa Hyman.

butter for greasing
4 thick, large slices of stale white sandwich bread, crust removed
2 tablespoons softened butter
2 tablespoons raisins
2 tablespoons currants
1 tablespoon mixed peel
grated rind of half a lemon
3 large eggs, beaten well
10 ounces whole milk
10 ounces table cream
3 tablespoons superfine sugar plus some extra
grated nutmeg or ground cinnamon
1 tablespoon melted butter
2 tablespoons brandy (optional)
confectioners' sugar (optional)
extra cream (optional)

Preheat the oven to 325°F. Butter a 9x13-inch baking dish.

Butter each slice of bread generously with the softened butter and cut into wide fingers. Layer one on top of the other in the buttered baking dish (the dish should be about half full), sprinkling the layers with the dried fruit, peel, and lemon zest.

Beat the eggs and add the milk, cream, sugar, and nutmeg or cinnamon.

Add the brandy if desired (but then it ceases to be Nursery Pudding!). Mix well and strain over the bread fingers.

Allow to stand for at least 30 minutes (preferably an hour), or until bread is well soaked.

Sprinkle the top with a little extra sugar and brush with the melted butter.

Place pan in a larger baking pan filled two-thirds full of boiling water. Bake for 40 minutes, or until firm to the touch. If desired sprinkle with confectioners' sugar and serve hot. Some people serve this with extra cream.

Serves 4.

Brioche Bread Pudding with Italian Orange Pastry Cream

Brioche is a light but rich French bread, almost like a cake. The word *brioche* has been in use since at least the fifteenth century. The quality of the butter used is what determines the quality of the brioche. The idea of preparing it with the Italian Pastry Cream came from Amy Riolo, a fabulous cook and food writer.

1/4 cup unsalted butter, room temperature
stale brioche (or challah), cut into 1/2-inch thick slices then in half into
    triangular shapes
2 cups milk
4 large eggs
1/4 cup sugar
1 teaspoon vanilla
pinch of salt

Italian Orange Pastry Cream

2 cups milk
6 large egg yolks
6 tablespoons sugar
zest of 1 orange
1/4 cup flour

Preheat oven to 350°F. Butter a 9x13-inch baking dish.

Butter the pieces of brioche. Layer brioche in the prepared baking dish at a 45-degree angle, so points are up.

In a large mixing bowl, mix together the milk, eggs, sugar, vanilla, and salt. Pour over pieces of brioche. Let stand 20 minutes. Custard should soak into the brioche, and points should be above the custard line.

Place the baking dish into a larger pan filled with hot water that comes about half way up the sides of the baking pan.

Bake until custard is set and brioche points are toasted, about 45 minutes. Meanwhile, prepare sauce.

In a medium saucepan over medium heat, bring milk to a boil. Remove pan from heat.

In a large mixing bowl, beat egg yolks, sugar, and orange zest until pale yellow in color, about 5 minutes.

Beat in the flour on low speed just until incorporated.

Slowly and carefully whisk in the hot milk, beating constantly. Pour into a large saucepan and cook over medium heat, stirring constantly for 4 to 5 minutes.

Do not allow mixture to boil.

Pastry cream is done when it coats the back of a spoon. You should be able to run your finger down the middle of the spoon without having the sides run. Cream may be served cold or hot. Makes about 2 cups of cream. Serve with bread pudding.

Serves 8.

Capirotada (Mexican Bread Pudding)

Capirotada usually has layers of nuts, cheese, dried or fresh fruit, and a cinnamon-sugar syrup. It is believed to have originated as a dish for Lent. In Mexico and Arizona this was originally made with *pinones*, or pine nuts, and in some recipes the bread cubes were fried before use in the recipe, like *Torrijas*.

Like *Torrijas*, this bread pudding has no custard base. It has a taste similar to apple pie with cheddar cheese!

canola spray for greasing
2 to 3 ounces tequila
1/2 cup golden raisins, divided
2 cups water
2 cinnamon sticks, or if available 1/2 teaspoon Mexican cinnamon and 1 cinnamon stick
1/2 cup sugar
1 long thin loaf stale French bread, sliced in 1/2-inch to 1-inch thick slices, and cubed1/2 cup golden raisins, divided
1 cup pine nuts, or pecans (or half and half), divided
3 large Granny Smith apples, peeled and diced, divided
2 cups grated cheddar cheese (or Monterey Jack), divided

Preheat oven to 350°F. Coat a 9x13-inch baking pan with canola spray.
Place raisins in a bowl with tequila.
In a quart pot, boil the water and cinnamon for 4 minutes, then stir in sugar, boil for another minute, then reduce heat and simmer for 5 minutes.
Remove cinnamon stick(s) and set aside.
Make a layer of bread cubes in the prepared pan. Sprinkle with half the raisins, then half the nuts, half the apples, and half the cheese.
Repeat making another layer of bread, raisins, nuts, apples, and cheese.
Pour sugar syrup over the top of the layered ingredients. Cover with aluminum foil.
Bake 45 minutes, remove from heat and let cool for 15 to 20 minutes.
Serves 8 to 12.

Challah Bread Pudding with Carrot Crème Anglaise

The drier the bread the better this dish, resulting in a crispy top, a tender inside, and bread pudding that tastes good warm or chilled. This recipe is from *PAR FORK!* by Gwen Ashley Walters, courtesy of the Bandon Dunes Golf Resort on the rugged Oregon coast. My friend Amy Riolo made this the night before Thanksgiving and served it for breakfast at a brunch buffet.

1 teaspoon butter, room temperature
5 cups heavy cream
5 large egg yolks
1 & 1/2 cups sugar
2 tablespoons (1 ounce) almond paste or 1/2 teaspoon almond extract
1 teaspoon vanilla
1/2 teaspoon cinnamon
1/4 teaspoon ground nutmeg
1 loaf (1 pound) stale challah cut into 1-inch cubes
1/3 cup dried cranberries

Carrot Crème Anglaise

3 cups fresh carrot juice
2 cups heavy cream
1 teaspoon ground cardamom
1 teaspoon vanilla
9 large egg yolks
1 & 3/4 cups sugar

Preheat oven to 350°F. Spread the butter all over the bottom and sides of a 9x13x2-inch baking pan.

Whisk together the cream and egg yolks, then whisk in the sugar, almond paste, vanilla, cinnamon, and nutmeg, whisking until sugar and almond paste dissolve.

Place the bread cubes all over the prepared baking pan. Sprinkle the cranberries evenly on top.

Pour the cream mixture over the bread, making sure each cube is moistened.

Soak at room temperature for about 10 minutes.

Set the pan in a larger pan in the oven and pour in enough hot water into the larger pan to come half way up the sides of the bread pan.

Bake until a knife inserted in the center comes out almost clean (about 50 to 60 minutes). The center should jiggle just a little.

Cool slightly and serve with Carrot Crème Anglaise, or cool completely and refrigerate. Warm before serving.

Serves 8 to 10.

Prepare sauce:

Bring carrot juice to a boil in a 2-quart saucepan over medium-high heat. Reduce until only 1/3 cup is left, about 30 minutes. The mixture will smell like it's starting to caramelize and will create a lot of foam. Cool to room temperature.

Bring cream, cardamom, and vanilla just to a boil in a saucepan over medium-high heat. Remove from heat.

Whisk egg yolks with sugar and reduced carrot juice until smooth.

Slowly drizzle a little of the hot cream mixture into the egg yolks, whisking constantly to prevent the eggs from cooking.

Stir the warmed eggs back into the remaining hot cream mixture.

Place the saucepan over medium-low heat. Cook, stirring frequently, until the sauce is thickened, about 20 minutes. If you run your FINGER across the back of the spoon, the path your finger creates should stay clean. If the sauce runs through the path, it is not thick enough and needs to cook a little longer. Do not allow to boil. Sauce should be reduced by 1/3 and foam removed from the top.

Remove from heat and cool.

Strain sauce into a bowl THEN set THAT bowl in a larger bowl of ice water to chill, stirring occasionally while cooling. Sauce may be made 1 day in advance. Refrigerate in a covered container. Sauce is a great accompaniment to a warm rice pudding or even a slice of yellow pound cake, but it's best over the Challah Bread Pudding.

Makes 3 cups.

Chocolate Cherry Croissant Bread Pudding

What combination could be better than chocolate and cherries! This is a quick, easy, and elegant dessert.

1 teaspoon butter
3 stale croissants
1/3 cup semi-sweet chocolate chips
1/3 cup dried cherries
1/3 cup sugar
1 cup cream
2 large eggs
1 tablespoon Cassis (or vanilla)

Generously butter a 9x9-inch baking dish.

Cut croissants into 1/2-inch pieces (as best you can) and scatter cubes, chips and cherries into prepared baking dish.

In a large bowl whisk together sugar, cream, eggs, and Cassis until sugar dissolves.

Pour sugar/cream mixture through a sieve into prepared baking dish.

Gently push down cubes so they absorb the egg mixture. Cover and refrigerate 30 minutes.*

Preheat oven to 350°F.

Bake for 40 minutes or until center is puffy and golden. Serve hot.

Serves 6.

*If in a rush, skip chilling. Instead pour only half of egg mixture in, push down to absorb; wait five minutes before pouring on some more but not all, leaving tops of cubes just above liquid line.

Chocolate-Chocolate Bread Pudding with White Chocolate Sauce

This recipe is a chocoholic's dream. Don't omit the whipped cream as it softens the intensity of so much chocolate. Another favorite of Marie Huntington, from her book *Cooks & Company*.

butter for greasing pan
2 tablespoons unsalted butter, melted
4 large eggs, lightly beaten
1 cup firmly packed dark brown sugar
3 cups heavy cream
1 cup milk
1 teaspoon vanilla
1/2 teaspoon cinnamon
1 cup melted milk chocolate
6 cups cubed stale bread
12 ounces bittersweet chocolate

White Chocolate Sauce

8 ounces white chocolate, chopped
1 cup heavy cream

Garnish:
Whipped cream
Fresh mint leaves
Confectioners' sugar
Cocoa powder

Preheat oven to 350°F. Grease 12 (1/2 cup) muffin tins.

In a mixing bowl, whisk together the butter, eggs, sugar, cream, milk, vanilla, cinnamon, and milk chocolate.

Fold in the bread cubes and spoon 1/2 cup of the mixture into each muffin tin.

Cut or break bittersweet chocolate into 12 cubes and press a chocolate cube into the center of each pudding.

Bake for 35 minutes or until the puddings are set.

Prepare White Chocolate Sauce. In the top of a double-boiler over simmering water, whisk the chocolate and cream until sauce is combined well. Do not let the mixture overheat. Makes 1 & 1/2 cups sauce.

Invert puddings and place each on a plate. Drizzle with White Chocolate Sauce, garnish with whipped cream and a dusting of confectioners' sugar and/or cocoa powder.

Makes 12 servings.

Chocolate Fig Bread Pudding
with Spirited Sauce

"Bring us some figgy pudding, oh bring us figgy pudding, oh bring us some figgy pudding and bring it here soon." I don't know what the figgy pudding of old was but this one will have you singing! The marriage of chocolate and figs is great, and the rum sauce just makes it better. This recipe is courtesy of the Valley Fig Growers of Fresno, California.

butter for greasing
4 cups stale white bread cut into 3/4-inch cubes
1 cup coarsely chopped dried Blue Ribbon Orchard Choice or Calimyrna
      California Figs (stems removed)
1/2 cup (3 ounces) chocolate morsels or coarsely chopped chocolate
2 cups milk
2 tablespoons butter
2 large eggs
1/4 cup sugar
2 teaspoons vanilla
1/4 teaspoon salt

Spirited Sauce

6 tablespoons butter
1 & 1/4 cup confectioners' sugar
1 large egg, beaten
1/4 cup dark rum or brandy

Preheat oven to 350°F. Grease a 1 & 1/2-quart baking dish or Pyrex bowl.
In a large bowl, combine the bread, figs, and chocolate. Place in prepared dish.
Heat the milk and butter in a pan until the butter is melted but do not let mixture boil.
Combine eggs, sugar, vanilla, and salt in a large mixing bowl.

Add hot milk mixture to the egg mixture stirring constantly. Pour over bread and fig mixture. Let stand 5 minutes.

Bake uncovered for 50 minutes or until a knife inserted in the center comes out clean.

If desired, baked pudding can be made several days ahead. Cover and refrigerate. Reheat in 325°F oven for 15 minutes.

Prepare Spirited Sauce:

For the sauce, combine butter and sugar in top part of double boiler.

Cook over simmering water until butter is melted, sugar is dissolved and mixture is very hot. Remove entire double boiler from the heat. Whisk beaten egg into sugar mixture. Remove the top of double boiler from bottom and continue beating until sauce has cooled to room temperature. Stir in rum or brandy to taste. Spoon pudding into dessert dishes and pass sauce separately.

Makes 4 to 6 servings.

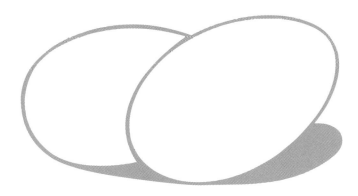

Chocolate Marmalade Croissant Bread Pudding

My friend, food writer and cooking instructor Amy Riolo, loves to make this dessert using Spanish *Pan de Leche* (sweet milk rolls) that she finds in the local supermarkets. Because not everyone has access to these rolls, she suggests using croissants if they are not available.

canola spray or canola margarine for greasing
12 ounces semi-sweet chocolate chips
4 tablespoons orange marmalade
3 stale croissants, split in half (or 6 *Pan de Leche* split in half)
4 large eggs
1 & 3/4 cups skim milk
2 cups heavy whipping cream
3 tablespoons brown sugar
1 teaspoon cinnamon

Grease a 9x13-inch baking pan.
Place the chocolate chips and marmalade in the top of a double boiler over simmering heat. Stir until chips are melted and mixed well with marmalade. Be careful not to burn the chocolate.
Place croissants or rolls cut side up in the bottom of the prepared pan.
With a spatula, carefully spread the chocolate/marmalade mixture over the croissants (or rolls) until they are evenly covered with chocolate mixture.
In a medium bowl, beat the eggs with a whisk. Add the milk, mixing well.
Add cream and whisk well to mix. Pour mixture evenly over bread in prepared pan.
Cover with plastic wrap and let sit for an hour at room temperature or overnight in the refrigerator.
Preheat oven to 350°F.
Uncover and sprinkle brown sugar and cinnamon evenly across the top.
Bake for 1 hour, remove from heat, and cool for 15 minutes. Serve warm or cool.
Serves 8 to 12.

Christmas Bread Pudding

A variety of pudding recipes, especially bread pudding, have been traditional Christmas dishes since the nineteenth century. Many of our current Christmas traditions, including culinary ones, can be traced back to Victorian times, England. In Charles Dickens's *A Christmas Carol*, Christmas dinner is highlighted by the presentation of Mrs. Cratchit's plum pudding, which Bob Cratchit proclaimed "the greatest success achieved by Mrs. Cratchit since their marriage."

This recipe comes from Dr. Mark Vogel, who is not only a psychologist, but also has a culinary degree from the Institute of Culinary Education. Although he still practices psychology, his deepest passion remains cooking (at an Italian/Mediterranean restaurant in New Jersey) and writing about food and wine. His column, "Food for Thought," is published in a number of New Jersey and Philadelphia newspapers and food-related websites.

Custard

1 quart half-and-half ("Yes, you can use regular milk, but c'mon, it's Christmas.")
1 cup sugar
1 tablespoon vanilla
6 large eggs
6 large egg yolks

Run cold water in a 2 & 1/2- to 3-quart pot, and pour it out.
Place the half-and-half and sugar in the pot and bring to a boil.
Meanwhile, whisk the eggs and egg yolks together in a large bowl.
When the milk has boiled SLOWLY pour the milk mixture into the eggs, in a thin stream, whisking CONSTANTLY. You can even pour it intermittently. If you pour it in too fast, you will scramble the eggs.
Add vanilla and mix well.
Strain mixture into a bowl and skim any foam off the surface. If you'd like, you can add some of your favorite liqueur to the custard now.

Bread Pudding

1/2 cup golden raisins
6 tablespoons melted butter
1/2 cup dried cherries
1/2 cup (or more) chocolate chips (optional)
6 ounces of stale French, Italian, or brioche bread cut into half-inch cubes
5 cups of the custard mixture

Preheat your oven to 300°F. Bring the raisins to a boil in water and then
    drain cubes.
In a large bowl, toss the bread cubes with the melted butter and then
    scatter them and the raisins, cherries, and chips (if using) into a
    1 & 1/2- to 2-quart baking dish.
Pour the custard over the bread. Press gently to moisten.
Now place the baking dish into a larger pan (such as a roasting pan). Pour
    hot tap water in the larger pan until it comes at least halfway up the
    outside of the baking dish. The purpose of the water bath is to cre-
    ate gentle and uniform heating. High oven temperatures and/or lack
    of insulation from the water can cause the custard to curdle.
Bake for 45 minutes to an hour or until the custard sets. The custard is set
    when it has a slight jiggle but is no longer fluid.
Serves 6 to 8.

    To avoid a scorched pot when boiling milk or making yogurt
wash the pot prior to use in cold water and don't dry it.

Dixie's Bread Pudding

This treatment was originally devised as a fancy French toast recipe at Sally Raphael's Bucks County Inn; but by increasing the amount of maple syrup called for, you get quite a delightful dessert. Preparation begins the day before baking.

butter for greasing
12 slices stale white bread
2 (8 ounces each) packages cream cheese, cubed
8 large eggs
2 cups milk
2/3 cup maple syrup
cinnamon

The day before serving, butter a 9x13-inch pan or casserole.
Remove crusts from bread, and cut bread into cubes.
Place half the cubes in prepared pan and add cream cheese cubes.
Top with remaining bread. In large bowl, with a wire whisk, beat the eggs, milk, and maple syrup.
Pour over bread. Sprinkle with cinnamon, cover, and refrigerate overnight.
The next day, preheat the oven to 375°F and bake, uncovered, for 45 minutes.
Serve warm with additional maple syrup if desired.
Serves 6 to 8.

Before measuring syrup, jelly, molasses, honey, or other sticky substances, lightly grease the measuring cup or spoon before measuring.

Dominic's Pumpkin Bread Pudding with Caramel Sauce

No, it's not made with pumpkin bread—just day-old bread and pureed pumpkin, but it's rich, fragrant, and addictive. Dominic Mobley is a sought-after caterer in Danville, Virginia, who owns Dominic's Waterside Grill. The casual restaurant is known for, among other things, its devilishly good desserts, including this pudding. This recipe is from *The Best of Virginia Farms Cookbook & Tourbook*, by food and travel writer CiCi Williamson, who is also the host of a PBS-TV series based on the book.

butter for greasing
3 large eggs
1 cup packed dark brown sugar
15-ounce can 100% pure pumpkin
1 tablespoon pumpkin-pie spice (if not available make your own)*
1 tablespoon cinnamon
1 tablespoon vanilla
2 cups half-and-half
4 cups cubed stale white bread, (pack the cubes in the cup when measuring—if you just lightly fill the cups, it's not enough bread to take up the liquid)
Caramel Sauce (recipe follows or use ready made/store bought)

* Pumpkin Pie Spice

Mix together:
2 teaspoons of cinnamon
1 teaspoon of ground ginger
1/2 teaspoon of ground allspice or ground cloves
1/2 teaspoon of ground nutmeg
Makes 1 tablespoon of pumpkin pie spice.

Preheat oven to 350°F. Butter a 2-quart rectangular glass baking dish; set aside.

In a large mixing bowl, with a whisk, beat eggs lightly.

Whisk in sugar, making sure all lumps are dissolved.

Whisk in pumpkin, pie spice, cinnamon, and vanilla.

Blend in half-and-half and bread and pour into prepared dish.

Bake 30 to 40 minutes, or until pudding reaches 160 to 165°F as measured in the center with a food thermometer.

Serve warm with warm Caramel Sauce.

Serves 8 to 10.

Caramel Sauce

1/2 cup butter
1 cup packed dark brown sugar
1 cup heavy cream

Place butter and brown sugar in a heavy-bottomed saucepan over medium heat. Stir until butter melts. Add cream and heat until sugar dissolves and sauce thickens slightly.

Makes about 2 cups sauce.

Inn at Little Washington's Custard Bread Pudding with Two Sauces

Patrick O'Connell is the chef/owner of the Inn and author of *The Inn at Little Washington Cookbook: A Consuming Passion*. His inspired American cuisine, which has been described by critics as "so good it makes you cry," draws admirers from around the world.

Patrick's approach to cooking, while paying homage to the lawmakers of Classical French Cuisine, reflects a belief in "the cuisine of today," healthy, eclectic, imaginative, unrestricted by ethnic boundaries, and always growing. He also takes great pleasure in taking the flavors from childhood, rediscovering the flavors and refining their combinations to make them new again. This recipe for Bread Pudding is a perfect example of this technique.

Patrick has been referred to as "the Pope of American Haute Cuisine." Selecting the Inn at Little Washington as one of the top ten restaurants in the world, Patricia Wells of the *International Herald Tribune* hails O'Connell as "a rare chef with a sense of near perfect taste, like a musician with perfect pitch." The Inn at Little Washington was created by Patrick O'Connell and his partner, Reinhardt Lynch in 1978. It became America's first five-star country house hotel and the first establishment in the *Mobil Travel Guide's* history to ever receive two five-star awards—for its restaurant and for its accommodations.

Bread Pudding

butter for greasing
1/3 ounce currants or golden raisins
about 1/3 cup warm bourbon
1 to 2 tablespoons unsalted butter
2 cups half-and-half
small piece vanilla bean
4 large eggs
1/2 cup sugar
1/2 loaf stale French bread,
    (about 3 1-ounce each
     slices per mold), sliced thin

Bourbon Caramel Sauce

1/4 cup sugar
3 tablespoons heavy cream, scalded
1 teaspoon unsalted butter
1 to 2 tablespoons bourbon

In a small bowl, soak the currants in bourbon for about 15 minutes, then drain.

Preheat oven to 350°F. Butter 6 (8 ounce each) metal or porcelain ramekins.

Combine half-and-half and vanilla bean and bring to a boil in a small saucepan.

Whisk eggs and sugar together in a bowl and slowly pour the hot liquid over them while continually whisking. Remove the vanilla bean.

Dip the bread into the custard mixture and then line the buttered molds with the moistened bread.

Sprinkle a few currants into each mold and fill with the custard mixture.

Place the molds in a large roasting pan filled with enough simmering water to bring the level halfway up the sides of the molds.

Bake for 45 minutes, remove from water bath, and allow to rest for 10 minutes.

To make the Bourbon Caramel Sauce combine the sugar and 3 tablespoons water in a heavy saucepan and cook until the mixture turns a dark caramel color.

Add the scalded heavy cream, stirring to mix well, add the butter and mix well, and when butter is completely mixed in, stir in the bourbon.

Unmold the custards onto dessert plates and serve with Crème Anglaise swirled with caramel sauce. You may only need to use half the Crème Anglaise.

Serves 6.

Crème Anglaise

4 large egg yolks
1/4 cup sugar
1/2 vanilla bean, split
zest of 1/2 lemon
2 cups half-and-half

To prepare Crème Anglaise, whisk the egg yolks and sugar in a bowl until light and fluffy.

Add the vanilla bean, lemon zest, and half-and-half.

In a double boiler over simmering water, cook, stirring constantly, until thickened. Remove the vanilla bean and chill the mixture.

Lemon Meringue Bread Pudding

This recipe is adapted from a recipe of Linda Wolfe's from her *Old-Fashioned Bread Puddings & Other Old-Fashioned Desserts* cookbook. Since it reminded me of Lemon Meringue Pie, I decided to "ice" it with meringue! (See www.bearwallowbooks.com for a catalog of their books.)

2 cups milk
1/2 cup heavy whipping cream
2 tablespoons butter
3/4 cup sugar
1/4 teaspoon salt
4 large eggs, separated
1/2 cup fresh squeezed lemon juice
3 cups stale challah bread cubes (about 5 slices of 1/2-inch thick challah)
grated zest of 2 lemons
fresh grated nutmeg

Meringue Topping

4 large egg whites
1/4 teaspoon cream of tartar (optional)
1/2 cup sugar

Preheat oven to 325°F. Butter a 9x13-inch baking pan.

Rinse a 2-quart pot in cold water (do not dry it). Place milk and cream in the pot and scald it. Remove from heat, stir in butter, and stir until melted. Blend in sugar and salt. Set aside to cool slightly.

In a medium-size bowl, beat the egg yolks with the lemon juice.

Stir or whisk in a half a cup of the hot milk mixture into the egg mixture. Set aside.

With your mixer, beat the egg whites until soft peaks form and whites are stiff.

Fold whites into the custard mixture.

Spread bread cubes in prepared pan. Sprinkle with grated lemon zest.

Pour the custard mixture over the bread cubes and carefully distribute it
evenly with a rubber spatula.

Sprinkle the top with a little fresh grated nutmeg.

Place baking pan in a larger pan with enough hot water to come almost
half way up the sides of the bread pudding pan.

Bake for 50 to 60 minutes until a knife inserted near the center comes
out clean. Prepare meringue while bread pudding is baking.

Using a mixer, beat egg whites with cream of tartar if needed, and gradually add sugar and beat until stiff peaks form.

Remove bread pudding from oven, raise oven temperature to 350°F. Ice
the top of the bread pudding with the meringue and return pudding to oven for 10 to 12 minutes or until meringue is lightly brown
on top.

Serve cool or cold.

Serves 8 to 12.

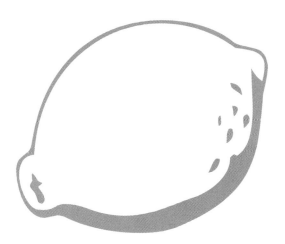

New Mexico Bread Pudding

Beth Hensperger has been educating, writing, and demo-lecturing about the art of baking bread for thirty years. She describes bread baking as "an art with only a few tools." Deeply spiritual and an avid student by nature, her quest for recipes has led her into many varied countries and communities to study culinary traditions, local history, and religious practices intertwined with food.

Hensperger is the best-selling author of fourteen cookbooks on the art of bread baking. Other books of interest include *Bread for All Seasons*, with recipes and text reflecting her interest in old European seasonal agricultural cycles and Colonial folklore, and *Breads of the Southwest*, a collection of modern recipes focusing on Native American and Hispanic contributions to the present-day American culinary arts. This recipe is from her book *Breads of the Southwest* (Chronicle Books).

Brown sugar is a classic ingredient in Mexican desserts and is usually found molded in the form of *piloncillos*. Serve this with a cream brandy sauce or just plain yogurt.

1 loaf stale homemade white bread or 12 slices stale French bread* cut
    into 1/2-inch slices and torn into large pieces
1-pound longhorn cheddar cheese thickly shredded OR 1 cup cheddar
    and 1 cup cream cheese
1/2 cup golden raisins or chopped dried figs, soaked for 15 minutes in
    warm water and drained
1/2 cup pine nuts or chopped pecans
2 cups light brown sugar
6 cups water
1 tablespoon vanilla
1 tablespoon cinnamon
pinch of ground cloves
2 tablespoons unsalted butter

Preheat oven to 350°F. Lightly grease a 9x13-inch baking pan.
Toast the bread in a 350°F oven for 10 minutes. Remove from oven and
    set aside.

In the prepared pan, place all the bread, cover it with all the cheese, sprinkle on all the raisins, then all the nuts.

In a 3-quart saucepan place the brown sugar, water, vanilla, cinnamon, and cloves.

Boil, stirring constantly to dissolve the sugar. Reduce heat to simmer and cook uncovered, stirring occasionally, for 10 to 15 minutes.

Add the butter and stir to melt. Pour the hot syrup over the top layer, evenly soaking everything.

Press down lightly to let the bread soak up the entire amount of syrup.

Cover with foil and bake in the center of the oven for 50 minutes to 1 hour or until firm. Serve warm or room temperature.

Serves 8.

Variation:

Beth suggests that you can pour the caramel over the bread, then layer the cheese, raisins, nuts on top.

*You can also use cinnamon rolls or old croissants.

Om 'Ali (Egyptian Bread and Butter Pudding)

I first had the pleasure of eating this many years ago in Egypt where the dessert is thought to have originated. I enjoyed it so much, I ate it every day! It has become popular throughout the Arab world as a traditional Eid al-Fitr sweet.

Amy Riolo, food writer and lecturer (she's an expert on Egyptian culture and cuisine), told me this story about the origin of the name. Descendants of the great Saladin ruled Egypt after him, and in 1249 Shagar al-Din, a woman, ruled as Sultana of Egypt. She convinced one of her officials to leave his wife (known as Umm Ali—Ali's mother) and marry her instead. Later, in a fit of jealousy, Shagar-al Din murdered her husband and to top it off, Umm Ali had her servants kill Shagar-al Din! Umm Ali gave her name to this dessert because the pleasure of eating it is akin to the sweetest revenge! There are as many spellings of the name as there are variations. It is sometimes spelled Um, Omm, or Umm Ali.

The Egyptian version uses roqaq, a type of cracker bread, or phyllo dough, but for most cooks, it is easier to use croissants. The Egyptians also use a variety of mixed nuts, including almonds, hazelnuts, pecans, and roasted peeled peanuts. A mixture of two or more nuts are used, which are then crushed very fine and mixed with sugar at a ratio of 2/3 nuts to 1/3 sugar. Rose water or vanilla is sometimes added.

butter for greasing
5 large stale croissants
1/4 to 1/3 cup shredded coconut
1/3 cup golden raisins
1/3 cup chopped walnuts
2 teaspoons cinnamon (optional)
1/2 cup sugar
2 cups whole milk
1 teaspoon vanilla or orange blossom water
1/2 cup cream, half-and-half, or whole milk
1/4 cup chopped pistachio nuts

Preheat oven to 250°F. Grease a 9x13-inch baking pan.
Tear croissants into small pieces and arrange on large baking sheet.

Place in oven for 20 minutes, or until well dried out.

Remove from oven and let cool slightly. Increase oven temperature to 350°F.

Place croissant pieces in large bowl and add coconut, raisins, walnuts, cinnamon, and sugar, mixing well.

In small saucepan, bring milk to boiling and stir in vanilla. Pour over croissant mixture, mix well, and let stand 10 minutes.

Pour mixture into prepared pan and pour cream on top.

Bake until cream begins to set and turn golden brown, about 15 minutes.

Sprinkle with pistachios and serve warm.

Serves 8.

Orange-Spice Rhubarb Betty

This recipe was contributed by Nancy Baggett, food journalist, researcher, and author of numerous popular and acclaimed cookbooks, including, most recently, *The All-American Dessert Book*. Nancy says that betties are homey American creations dating back to the nineteenth century. They were probably devised to use up leftover bread and may have evolved from bread puddings. She says it's the inclusion of bread or cracker crumbs that distinguishes them from crisps and cobblers. No one seems to know where the name "betty" came from.

Early betties were layered in deep dishes and were rather pudding-like, but modern recipes such as this one are usually baked in a shallow pan, so the top crisps and the fruit juices concentrate.

In Nancy's recipe, ginger, cinnamon, and orange zest round out the zesty rhubarb flavor and aroma, and a buttery topping adds richness and a slight crunch.

3/4 cup all-purpose white flour
1/2 cup packed light brown sugar
1/8 teaspoon salt
1/2 cup (1 stick) unsalted butter, melted (divided use)
scant 1 cup granulated sugar
3/4 teaspoon ground cinnamon
3/4 teaspoon ground ginger
2/3 cup orange juice
3/4 teaspoon finely grated orange zest (orange part of the skin)
6 & 1/2 cups 3/4-inch rhubarb cubes (2 to 2 & 1/2 pounds well-trimmed stalks)
4 cups 1/3-inch cubes of good quality stale crusty sourdough, French, or firm, rustic-style bread (removing crust is optional)

Place a rack in the upper third of the oven and preheat to 375°F. Lightly grease or spray a 9x13-inch (or similar) rectangular flat baking dish with nonstick spray.

In a medium bowl, thoroughly stir together the flour, brown sugar, and salt. Add half the butter (no need to measure exactly). With forks or a pastry cutter, work in the butter until evenly incorporated. Set the flour mixture and remaining butter aside.

In a large bowl, stir together granulated sugar, cinnamon, ginger, orange juice, and orange zest until blended. Add the rhubarb, bread, and reserved butter, tossing until well mixed. Spread 1/2 cup of the flour mixture in the baking dish. Spread the rhubarb mixture evenly over top. Sprinkle the remainder of the flour mixture evenly over the rhubarb.

Bake on the upper rack for 45 to 50 minutes, or until the betty is bubbly, well browned, and crisp on top. (It's better to overbake than underbake.) Transfer to wire rack. Let cool at least 15 minutes before serving. Serve warm, garnished with a scoop of light vanilla ice cream or frozen yogurt, if desired.

This may be kept, covered and refrigerated, up to 3 days. Let warm to room temperature or reheat to warm in a low oven before serving.

Makes 8 or 9 servings.

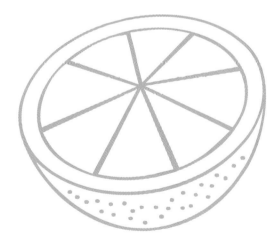

Peach Melba Bread Pudding with Raspberry Sauce

Two elements of a classic peach melba (peaches and raspberries) reappear in this treatment, which is festive enough to serve to special guests. This is a wonderful choice for a simple brunch dish and tastes just as good the next day as the day it is prepared.

12 ounces cream cheese, softened
1 cup sugar
6 large eggs
1 & 1/2 cups milk
3/4 teaspoon almond extract
1 & 1/2 teaspoons grated lemon peel
1 & 1/2 teaspoons vanilla
5 & 1/4 cups stale bread cubes (cut in 1/2-inch cubes)
29-ounce can peach halves, well drained, plus 14-ounce can (peaches in juice are fine)
5 tablespoons seedless raspberry jam
6 teaspoons sugar combined with 1/2 teaspoon cinnamon and 6 tablespoons sliced almonds

Raspberry Sauce

(optional)
1 (10-ounce) package frozen raspberries, thawed
2 teaspoons cornstarch
1 tablespoon seedless raspberry jam
1 teaspoon of lemon juice

Preheat oven to 325°F.
In large bowl, with mixer on medium, beat cream cheese and sugar until smooth.

Add eggs and beat until blended. At low speed, beat in milk, almond extract, lemon peel, and vanilla.

Place bread cubes in greased 12x7-inch baking pan and pour egg mixture on top.

Place peach halves, cut side up, on top, gently pressing down on the peaches so they are nestled in the pudding instead of perched on top, making sure no egg mixture flows into center of peach halves.

Spoon 1 teaspoon of raspberry jam into each peach center. Sprinkle with sugar-cinnamon mixture and top with almonds.

Bake 40 minutes, or until pudding is set. Turn oven to broil and let top brown slightly.

For the sauce, puree thawed raspberries and their liquid; press through a sieve to remove seeds. In small saucepan combine cornstarch with pureed raspberries and cook, stirring, until thickened and bubbly. Remove from heat, and stir in jam and lemon juice. Let cool slightly.

Serve with warm sauce if desired.

Serves 8.

Persimmon Bread Pudding

Recently I acquired *Old Fashioned Bread Puddings & Other Old-Fashioned Desserts,* a little book from Bear Wallow Books (publishers of small books of old-fashioned recipes). They were gracious enough to share their Persimmon Bread Pudding. The dessert is nice as well as spicy, and tastes great the next day. My friend Sharon suggests serving it with a big cup of café au lait! Like most persimmon puddings, this one has a thick, cake-like consistency and is best cut into squares and served warm.

butter for greasing
1/4 cup butter, softened
1/2 cup sugar
1/2 cup brown sugar
3 large eggs, beaten
1 teaspoon vanilla
1/4 teaspoon salt
1/2 teaspoon baking soda
1 teaspoon cinnamon
1/2 teaspoon ground ginger
1/2 teaspoon allspice
1 cup whole milk
1 cup persimmon pulp (available frozen in some places)
2 cups stale 3/4-inch crustless bread cubes
1/2 cup chopped nuts (optional)
nutmeg

Preheat the oven to 350°F. Butter an 8-inch square baking pan.

In a large mixing bowl, cream the butter and sugars. Blend in the eggs beaten with the vanilla.

Add the salt, baking soda, and spices. Alternately stir in the milk, persimmon pulp, and bread cubes, blending well. Fold in the nuts (if using) and pour the batter into the prepared pan. Dash a little nutmeg on the top, cover the pan with aluminum foil, and bake for 30 to 35 minutes.

Remove the foil and bake 15 to 20 minutes more. Pudding tests done when a knife inserted in the center of the pudding comes out clean.

Serves 6.

Pioneer Bread Pudding with Lemon Sauce

butter for greasing
2 cups stale bread cubes (1/4- to 1/2-inch pieces), crusts removed
2 cups milk
1/4 cup sugar
3 tablespoons butter
2 large eggs
pinch of salt
1/2 teaspoon vanilla

Lemon Sauce

1 cup sugar
2 tablespoons cornstarch
1/8 teaspoon salt
1 tablespoon grated lemon peel
1/4 cup butter
2 tablespoons fresh lemon juice

Garnish:
whipped cream and lots of it (It is a nice foil for the lemon sauce.)

Preheat oven to 350°F. Grease a 1-quart baking dish.
Place the bread cubes in prepared baking dish.
In a large saucepan, over medium-low heat, combine the milk, sugar, and
    butter. Heat, stirring until sugar is dissolved and butter melts in the
    warm milk. Mixture should be warm, not too hot.
In a small bowl, beat the eggs slightly with the salt, and stir into the warm
    milk mixture. Add vanilla and mix well. Remove from heat and pour
    over bread cubes.
Place the baking dish in a larger pan and fill the larger pan with enough
    hot water to come half-way up the outside of the baking dish.
Bake for an hour, or until a knife inserted in the center comes out clean
While bread pudding is baking prepare lemon sauce.

Combine the sugar, cornstarch, and salt in a medium saucepan.
Mix well, and stir in 2 cups water and lemon peel. Boil for 1 minute and
    remove from the heat. Stir or whisk in the butter and lemon juice.
Serve hot or cold with plain cream, or serve hot with lemon sauce.
Serves 4 to 6.

Southern Bread Pudding with Whiskey Sauce

Southerners have never stopped loving bread puddings, which are a familiar staple in many restaurants in New Orleans. This spirited dessert combines a classic bread pudding with a zesty whiskey sauce. If you'd rather not indulge, you can serve the pudding with vanilla ice cream or frozen yogurt.

1 loaf stale French bread
1 quart milk
1/4 cup unsalted butter, softened
3 large eggs
1 & 1/3 cups sugar
2 tablespoons vanilla
1 cup raisins

Whiskey Sauce

1/2 cup unsalted butter
1 cup sifted confectioners' sugar
1 large egg, well beaten
1/4 cup bourbon whiskey, or to taste

Preheat oven to 325°F. Spray-coat a 9x13-inch baking dish.
For the pudding, crumble bread into large bowl.
Over low heat, or in microwave, heat milk and butter until butter melts.
Pour milk mixture over bread and let stand 45 minutes.
In small bowl, beat together eggs, sugar, vanilla and stir into bread mixture.
Add raisins, mix well, and pour in bread mixture.
Bake 1 hour and 10 minutes, or until browned and set.
Let cool slightly while preparing sauce.
For the sauce, combine butter and sugar in top part of double boiler.
Cook over simmering water until butter is melted, sugar is dissolved, and mixture is very hot.

Remove entire double boiler from the heat. Whisk beaten egg into sugar mixture. Remove the top of double boiler from bottom and continue beating until sauce has cooled to room temperature.

Stir in bourbon to taste. Spoon pudding into dessert dishes and pass sauce separately.

Serves 6 to 8.

Southwest Bread Pudding with Tequila Sauce

On my first trip to Santa Fe, over thirty-five years ago, I had this bread pudding in a well-known restaurant. This is an adaptation of their fabulous bread pudding. If you would like to serve this with rum sauce instead of Tequila Sauce, eliminate the lime juice and substitute rum. This can be made "low fat" by substituting egg-beaters, a light butter, skim evaporated milk, and 1/4 cup less sugar.

butter for greasing
1/2 pound stale French bread
1 cup milk
8 tablespoons butter or margarine, melted
1/2 cup golden raisins
1/3 cup pine nuts
3 large eggs, beaten or an egg substitute
1 & 1/4 cups sugar
1/4 cup dark brown sugar
4-ounce can skim evaporated milk
8.25-ounce can (or you can use a larger can) crushed pineapple with
    juice
1 teaspoon fresh lemon juice
3 teaspoons vanilla

Tequila Sauce

1 cup sugar
1 large egg
1/4 pound butter, melted
1/3 cup good quality tequila (without the worm)
1 teaspoon lime juice

Preheat the oven to 350°F. Butter an 8x12-inch baking pan.
Break bread into bite-size chunks and soak it in the milk.
Squeeze the bread with your fingers to eliminate excess liquid and discard milk.

Place bread in a large bowl and add butter, raisins, pine nuts, eggs, sugars, milk, pineapple, lemon juice, and vanilla.

Very gently, mix thoroughly.

Pour mixture into prepared baking pan and bake for an hour or until a knife inserted in the center comes out clean.

While pudding is baking, prepare the sauce. Cream together the sugar and egg.

Add the butter and pour into a medium saucepan.

Over low heat, stir mixture until sugar is dissolved. Remove from heat and stir in tequila and lime juice.

Pour over servings of bread pudding. Pudding may be served warm or cold, and so can sauce. Serve with extra sauce.

Serves 10.

Torrijas/Sweet Toasts

According to author Janet Mendel, these toasts are much like "French toast," but in Spain they are served as dessert, not breakfast. Everywhere in La Mancha, *torrijas* are absolutely essential during Holy Week and Easter holidays. I wonder if this derives from the Jewish tradition of using up all of the *hametz*, or leavened bread, before Passover—the springtime festival that usually coincides with Holy Week. Possibly *conversos*, converts to Christianity, brought with them to a new religion some of the customs of the former. They are fried mostly in southern Spain, not in northern Spain. A nice option is to serve this with macerated berries.

12 slices stale bread or brioche (3/4 pound)
2 cups milk
1/2 cup sugar
1/4 cup red or white wine
1 piece of lemon peel
2 large eggs, well beaten
1/4 cup olive oil
1 teaspoon cinnamon
1 tablespoon sugar (or 2 tablespoons honey) heated with 1 tablespoon
    water

Macerated Berries

(optional)
1/4 cup sugar
2 & 1/2 tablespoons water
1 cup picked over berries (raspberries, blackberries, strawberries, or mixture)
1/2 tablespoon lemon juice
1/2 teaspoon minced fresh mint

Prepare berries:
In a small saucepan, bring sugar and water to a boil, stirring until sugar is

dissolved. Let cool, pour over berries in a medium-size bowl. Add lemon juice and mint. Let sit for an hour. Drain juices before serving.

To prepare *Torrijas*:

Place the slices of bread in one layer in a pan.

In a saucepan, heat the milk with the 1/2 cup sugar until sugar is dissolved. Remove from heat and add the wine and lemon peel to the milk.

Pour this liquid over the bread and allow to set until liquid is absorbed, about 10 minutes.

Place the beaten eggs in a dish.

Heat some of the oil in a large, heavy skillet.

Dip the slices of bread into the egg on both sides. Fry them until browned on both sides.

Remove to a platter.

When all the bread slices are fried, sprinkle them with cinnamon and sugar or honey that has been boiled 1 minute. Serve the toasts hot or cold.

Serves 6.

Torrijas a la Taberna del Alabardero

Executive Chef Santi Zabaleta of the well-known Washington restaurant Taberna del Alabardero told me that *Torrijas* translates to "Sponge Cake Soaked in Spiced Milk."

He also told me that in the south of Spain, wine is used because the region is poor and there is not a lot of dairy. *Torrijas* is now a popular year-round dessert found on the menus of most Spanish restaurants.

2 loaves fresh challah bread (loaf shape)
6 ounces large egg yolks
8 ounces sugar
3 cups whole milk
3 ounces unsalted butter
3 cups heavy cream
1/2 teaspoon nutmeg
1 cinnamon stick
1/2 vanilla bean

Garnish:
ground cinnamon
sugar
sprig of mint

Macerated Berries

(optional)
1/4 cup sugar
1 cup cleaned berries (raspberries, blackberries, strawberries, or mixture)
1/2 tablespoon lemon juice
1/2 teaspoon minced fresh mint

Cut bread into slices (2-inches thick), and trim crust off bread.
Place egg yolks and sugar in the top of a double boiler or in a bowl over

simmering water/water bath, and whisk until soft peaks are formed, about 5 minutes.

In a 3-quart saucepan, bring milk, butter, cream, nutmeg, cinnamon stick, and vanilla bean to a boil over high heat.

Slowly incorporate, whisking constantly, the heated milk/cream mixture into the egg yolk/sugar mixture, over medium heat, until mixture reaches a heavy cream consistency, about 3 to 4 minutes. Remove vanilla bean and cinnamon stick.

Pour hot mixture over the bread, and let the bread soak and cool. When cool, cover and refrigerate for 12 hours before serving.

Once the bread is chilled, serve in a bowl sprinkled with cinnamon and sugar. Garnish with sprig of mint.

If using berries, place sugar and 2 & 1/2 tablespoons water to boil in a small pan, stirring until sugar is dissolved. Let cool. Place berries in a bowl, pour syrup over berries, add lemon juice and mint. Let berries sit for an hour. Drain juices before serving.

Serves 10.

Tropical Bread Pudding with Bananas and Pineapple

The seductively sweet flavors of pineapple and banana along with a coconut-flavored meringue topping make this selection unique.

butter for greasing
4 thick slices stale white bread
2 tablespoons butter or margarine, softened
3 large eggs, separated
1 & 1/4 cups pineapple juice
1/4 + 1/3 cup sugar, divided
1 teaspoon vanilla, divided
3 medium bananas, sliced
8.25-ounce can crushed pineapple, with juice
1/4 teaspoon cream of tartar
shredded or grated coconut (optional for garnish)

Preheat oven to 350°F. Grease a 2-quart square baking dish.
Spread bread with butter and cut into small cubes; set aside. In large bowl, beat egg yolks until light.
Add pineapple juice, 1/4 cup sugar and 1/2 teaspoon of vanilla.
Stir in bread cubes, stirring just until moistened. In a small bowl, combine banana slices with pineapple and its juice, and place in bottom of prepared baking dish.
Cover with bread mixture and bake for 35 minutes.
For meringue, in medium bowl, with mixer on high, beat egg whites, remaining vanilla, and cream of tartar until soft peaks form.
Gradually add 1/3 cup of sugar, beating until stiff peaks form.
Spread over hot pudding, sealing to edges of baking dish. Sprinkle with coconut and bake 15 minutes longer. Serve warm.
Serves 6.

White and Dark Chocolate Bread Pudding with Irish Cream Sauce

Touted as an outstanding bread pudding by those who eat at Carmen Anthony's Steak Houses, in Connecticut, it is the perfect finishing touch. The liqueur-flavored sauce turns this rich dessert into something wonderfully decadent. When I asked Operations Director Mike, facetiously, if the pudding was fattening, he told me, "Nothing is fattening if eaten in moderation." So don't be afraid to dig into this scrumptious dessert.

Irish Cream Sauce

2 cups whipping cream
6 tablespoons Irish cream liqueur
1/4 cup sugar
1/2 teaspoon vanilla extract
2 teaspoons cornstarch

Bread Pudding

canola spray for greasing pan
14 cups 3/4-inch cubes stale French bread with crust (about 12 ounces)
6 ounces bittersweet (not unsweetened) or semi-sweet chocolate, chopped
6 ounces imported white chocolate, chopped
4 large eggs
1/2 cup plus 4 tablespoons sugar, divided
2 teaspoons vanilla extract
2 cups whipping cream, divided
1/2 cup whole milk

In a heavy, medium-size pan over medium-high heat, bring to a boil the cream, liqueur, sugar, and vanilla. Stir frequently with a wooden spoon.

Mix together the cornstarch and 2 teaspoons water in small bowl, then whisk mixture into cream sauce.

Boil until sauce thickens, stirring constantly, about 3 minutes.

Cool, then cover and refrigerate until cold (about 2 hours). Sauce can be prepared 3 days ahead but must be kept in the refrigerator.

Spray a 13x9x2-inch glass baking dish.

Combine bread and chocolates in large bowl, mixing well.

Using an electric mixer and a large bowl, beat together the eggs, 1/2 cup plus 2 tablespoons sugar, and vanilla. Gradually beat in 1 & 1/2 cups cream and milk. Add cream mixture to bread mixture; stir to combine. Let stand 30 minutes.

Preheat oven to 350°F.

Place bread mixture in prepared dish, spreading evenly.

Drizzle with remaining 1/2 cup cream.

Sprinkle with remaining 2 tablespoons sugar.

Bake pudding until edges are golden and custard is set in center (about 1 hour).

Cool pudding slightly. Drizzle bread pudding with sauce and serve warm.

Serves 8

White Chocolate Sundried Cherry Bread Pudding with Raspberry Coulis

When I first tasted this recipe from Phyllis Frucht, I thought I had died and gone to chocolate cherry heaven! This dessert is perfect for entertaining and/or holidays.

butter for greasing
1 cup sundried cherries
1/3 cup Kirsch, a cherry-flavored liqueur
4 cups stale Italian or French bread, cubed
3/4 cup sugar
1 pint milk
1 pint heavy cream
1 stick unsweetened butter, melted, cooled to room temperature
4 large eggs
1/2 pound white chocolate chunks
1 teaspoon vanilla

Preheat the oven to 400°F. Grease a 2 & 1/2- to 3-quart baking pan.

Combine the cherries and Kirsch in a small bowl and let stand until plumped, about an hour, mixing occasionally.

Combine the bread, sugar, milk, cream, melted butter and eggs in a large bowl and let stand for an hour.

Mash well with a fork and add the vanilla, cherries, Kirsch, and chocolate chunks.

Pour into prepared pan. Smooth the top and bake for 40 minutes or until a knife inserted comes out clean.

Serve warm or chilled or with Raspberry Coulis, or whipped cream if desired. Garnish with fresh raspberries.

Serves 8.

Raspberry Coulis

1 package frozen raspberries in heavy syrup, thawed
1 tablespoon lemon juice
1 tablespoon Kirsch

In processor or blender, puree the ingredients until smooth then strain to
remove seeds.

Fabulous French Toast

*F*rench toast has been defined as "a breakfast dish made by dipping bread into a milk-egg mixture, then frying it until golden brown on both sides. It's usually served with syrup, jam or confectioners' sugar. In England French toast is called 'poor knights of Windsor.' The French call it *pain perdu* (lost bread) because it is a way of reviving French bread, which becomes dry after only a day or two." (Barron's Educational Series, from the *New Food Lover's Companion,* by Sharon Herbst).

There are several conflicting stories about the origin of French toast. Some allege it is called French toast because it originated "across the pond," where inventive French cooks devised an appetizing way to deal with stale bread. Others say it is not of French origin at all since it does not stem from classical French cuisine. Toast it may be, they say, but "French" it is not! *The Accomplished Cook,* written in 1660 by R. May has a recipe for "French Toasts," which calls for French bread sliced and toasted, then soaked in wine, sugar, and orange juice, a far cry from our breakfast favorite.

Still another story traces the invention of French toast to a roadside tavern near Albany, New York, in 1724. According to the tale, Joseph French, the owner of the tavern, gave his name to this dish. Cajun cooks in Louisiana claim to have invented or brought French toast to this country based on their *pain perdu*. But in the end, whoever invented it, or however it arrived, French toast is here to stay. And not only for breakfast, either. According to *The Joy of Cooking*, while we eat French toast for breakfast, the French eat it for dessert!

The best French toast is plump slices of bread soaked in a rich mixture of eggs and cream, and cooked in unsalted butter until a honey-brown color and mildly crisp. In any French toast recipe, the most important element is the bread. There is a variety to choose from, but the best bread is always a hearty loaf (if possible a day or more old) that can stand up to prolonged soaking in the egg batter. French bread (baguette), sourdough bread, and challah (egg bread) are all excellent choices. Also of importance is the milk you mix with the eggs for soaking. Whenever possible use half-and-half, whole milk, or light cream (or a combination thereof). While low-fat milk might be healthier, it just makes the batter too watery.

Baked French Toast with Blueberries

Another French toast favorite from the annual brunch class of the students at Cooks & Company. I prepared this with dried blueberries and dried cherries. When made in the suggested baking pan, it is filled to the top, so I asked my tester, Kristen, to try it in a 9x13-inch pan (so the ingredients would be spread out a little more). She reported back that her family liked my "smushed in the pan" version better than hers.

butter for greasing
1 to 1 & 1/2 loaves of stale French bread, crust removed and sliced 3/4-inch thick*
8 large eggs
1 cup milk
3/4 teaspoon vanilla extract
1/2 cup butter, softened
1 cup brown sugar
1/4 cup all-purpose flour
1 cup rolled oats (not instant)
1 cup chopped walnuts
1 to 2 cups fresh blueberries, or dried blueberries, or dried blueberries and cherries

Preheat oven to 375°F. Grease a 7x11-inch baking pan.
Place bread slices in a single layer in the bottom of the prepared pan, and cut additional bread into small pieces to fill in spaces around the slices.
Beat eggs and milk together and add vanilla. Pour egg mixture over the bread (there should be enough liquid to cover bread. Add more milk if necessary).
Let the bread, egg, and milk mixture set one or two minutes to allow bread to absorb the egg mixture.
Turn bread slices to evenly soak on both sides.
Using a pastry blender or your fingers, blend together the butter, brown sugar, and flour. Stir in the oats. Spread the walnuts and blueberries over the soaked bread in the prepared baking dish.

Sprinkle or spread (using your fingers) oat mixture over all. Press gently down on the top. Place baking pan on a pizza pan or cookie sheet to catch any spills or overflow during baking.

Bake 30 to 40 minutes or until bread is puffy and bubbles rise around the sides of the pan. Remove from oven and let set for 5 minutes before cutting into squares to serve.

Makes 6 to 8 servings.

*I used two 6 1/2x3-inch individual French baguettes

Berries should be kept cold and dry at all times until used. Keep berries away from moisture and wash them just before using. Buy berries that are plump, dry, smooth, even-colored, and free of dents. Check berry package for leakage.

Citrus French Toast

The citrus flavoring in this recipe really takes French toast to a new level of taste.

From Linda Wolfe's *Old Fashioned Orange Grove Recipes*.

2 large eggs, slightly beaten
1/2 cup orange juice
2 teaspoons lemon juice
2 tablespoons sugar
2 teaspoons grated orange zest (rind)
dash salt
2 tablespoons butter
4 slices stale bread
orange slices
cinnamon

In a medium bowl, beat the orange juice and lemon juice into the eggs. Stir in the sugar, orange rind, and salt. Mix thoroughly.

Melt the butter in a large skillet. Immerse the bread in the egg mixture, turning to coat both sides.

Fry coated bread slices until golden brown on each side. Sprinkle with cinnamon.

Serve on hot plates and garnish with orange slices.

Serves 2 to 4.

Crème Brûlée French Toast

Crème Brûlée is a luxurious dessert made of eggs, heavy cream, and sugar, with a brown-sugar topping. This offering features a brown-sugar base, making syrup or other sweet toppings unnecessary. Your guests will be begging for more. Besides tasting fabulous, an added advantage is that the dish is prepared the day before, but baked right before serving.

canola spray
1/2 cup butter
1 cup brown sugar
2 tablespoons corn syrup
15 slices stale French bread or 6 thick slices stale country-style or egg
    bread
5 large eggs
1 & 1/2 cups half-and-half
1 teaspoon vanilla
1 teaspoon orange liqueur (such as Grand Marnier or Triple Sec)
1/4 teaspoon salt

Grease a 9x3-inch baking pan.
The day before serving, place butter, brown sugar, and corn syrup in a
    heavy saucepan over medium heat.
Cook until butter is melted and mixture is smooth. Pour into prepared
    baking pan.
Add bread slices, squeezing them slightly to fit in single layer if necessary.
In medium bowl, whisk together eggs, half-and-half, vanilla, orange li-
    queur, and salt. Pour over bread. Cover and refrigerate overnight.
Preheat oven to 350°F.
About 1 hour before serving, remove bread from refrigerator and let stand
    at room temperature for 30 minutes. Bake, uncovered, 30 to 35 min-
    utes, or until bread is puffy and egg mixture is set.
Serves 6 to 8.

Variation:
Similar, but a little different is the following Crème Caramel French Toast.

Crème Caramel French Toast

This mouth watering treat is also begun the day before baking and serving.

2 tablespoons corn syrup
1 cup dark brown sugar
1/2 cup butter
1 pound stale cinnamon raisin bread
6 large eggs
2 cups milk
2 cups light cream
1/3 cup sugar
1 tablespoon vanilla (or substitute part of vanilla with an orange liqueur)
1/2 teaspoon salt
sour cream, fresh berries (optional)

Combine the corn syrup, brown sugar, and butter in a saucepan over medium heat. Melt, stirring, until smooth and bubbly.

Spread on the bottom of a 9x13-inch glass baking dish. Overlap the bread (like dominoes) on the syrup.

In a large bowl, combine the eggs, milk, light cream, sugar, vanilla, and salt.

Pour the mixture over the bread and refrigerate overnight; don't worry about any extra liquid in the dish—it bakes up like custard.

Preheat oven to 350°F.

Cover pan with foil and bake for 45 minutes, remove foil and bake uncovered for another 15 minutes. The toasts should be puffed and golden.

Cut into 8 pieces and invert to serve. If desired, top with sour cream and fresh berries.

Serves 8 to 10.

Deep Dish Brioche French Toast

David Leite, publisher of the website Leite's Culinaria (http://www.leitesculinaria.com), wrote a wonderful article about brunch. I have to quote him because he is so eloquent, has a marvelous sense of humor, and is a great cook to boot. "The problem with being among the multitudes who consider Sunday morning the next best thing to a national holiday—hence our right to sleep late—is that few of us have the constitution to rouse ourselves to actually cook. The idea of stumbling out of bed clear-headed enough to wield sharp objects and making something that would astound friends is, quite frankly, foreign to us. That's why there are restaurants." David discovered this recipe while "loafing" at the Black Boar Inn, in Ogunquit, Maine. Besides the fabulous taste and texture, David was intrigued by the fact that the recipe can be prepared ahead and sit in the refrigerator overnight. He could then sleep late on Sunday and still have this dish ready in time for brunch.

butter for greasing
1 (24-ounce) stale brioche loaf, cut into 1-inch cubes
8-ounce package cream cheese, cut into 18 cubes
3/4 cup chopped pecans or walnuts
1/2 cup golden raisins
8 large eggs
2 cups milk
1/2 cup firmly packed dark brown sugar
2 teaspoons vanilla
1 teaspoon cinnamon
pinch of nutmeg
pinch of cloves
4 tablespoons melted butter

For serving:
confectioners' sugar
pure maple syrup, warmed

Generously butter a 9x3-inch baking dish. Place half the brioche cubes in the pan in a single layer, filling in all the gaps.

Evenly scatter the cream cheese cubes, nuts, and raisins over the top. Cover completely with the remaining brioche cubes.

In a large bowl, whisk together the eggs, milk, brown sugar, vanilla, cinnamon, nutmeg, and cloves.

Pour the egg mixture evenly over the brioche cubes.

Gently press down on the cubes with your palms to allow the top layer of brioche to absorb the liquid.

Cover with plastic wrap and refrigerate 4 hours or overnight.

Preheat the oven to 350°F. Remove the dish from the refrigerator and let sit at room temperature for 20 to 30 minutes. Bake uncovered for 30 minutes.

Remove from the oven, drizzle the melted butter on top, return to the oven, and bake until the cubes are nicely toasted and there is no liquid puddling on the bottom of the dish.

Remove to a rack and run the knife around the rim of the pan to release the French toast.

Cut into squares, arrange on individual plates, sprinkle with confectioners' sugar, and serve along with the warmed maple syrup.

Serves 6 to 8.

French Toast Sandwich Surprise

The surprise is a spoonful of berry preserves or warm melting chocolate inside each piece of French toast. If you like jelly doughnuts, you will love raspberry-filled French toast. Or if you like *pain au chocolat* (chocolate-filled croissants), this recipe also fills the bill.

Serve for breakfast or brunch with maple syrup, or for dessert with a scoop of rich vanilla ice cream. This is from cookbook author, food writer, and restaurateur Judy Zeider's book *The 30-Minute Kosher Cook*.

8 slices stale challah or white bread, about 1/2- inch thick, crusts removed
1/2 cup raspberry preserves (or 4 ounces semi-sweet chocolate, cut into
    1/2-inch chunks)
1 tablespoon water mixed with 1 tablespoon flour to make a paste
    (optional)
4 extra-large eggs
8 tablespoons milk
unsalted butter, for frying plus a tablespoon of canola oil
confectioners' sugar, for garnish (optional)

Cut the bread diagonally in half to form 16 triangles. Place 1 tablespoon
    preserves or a chunk of chocolate in the center of 8 of the triangles
    and brush the edges with the water-flour paste if desired. (I found it
    was not really necessary to do this.)
Cover with the remaining 8 triangles, pressing the edges together firmly
    to seal.
In a medium shallow bowl, whisk together the eggs and milk.
Dip each "sandwich" on both sides into the egg mixture just until moist.
In a large nonstick skillet, melt the butter over medium-high heat and
    sauté the "sandwiches" on both sides until golden brown.
To serve, arrange each triangle on a serving plate and sprinkle with con-
    fectioners' sugar.
Makes 8 servings

Variation:
Replace the preserves and chocolate with smoked salmon. Serve with sour cream or *creme fraiche* instead of maple syrup.

Maple French Toast

Patricia Allen, chef and owner of the Morning Star Inn B&B and cooking school, in Highlands, N.C., loves to serve this to her guests. The recipe is so popular, she included it in her book *Whisk Upon A Star: Morning Star Inn.*

18 slices stale white sandwich bread, cut into 1-inch cubes, crusts
    removed
8-ounce package cream cheese, softened
12 large eggs
2 cups half-and-half
1/2 cup maple syrup
1 teaspoon cinnamon

Place the bread cubes in a lightly greased 9x13x2-inch baking dish and
    set aside.
Beat the cream cheese at medium speed in an electric mixer, until smooth.
Add the eggs, half-and-half, maple syrup, and cinnamon, beating until
    well blended.
Pour over the bread cubes, cover, and refrigerate 8 hours or overnight.
Preheat oven to 375°F.
Remove "French Toast" from the refrigerator. Let stand at room tempera-
    ture for 30 minutes.
Bake for 40 to 50 minutes or until set, covering with foil after 25 minutes.
Serve with additional syrup.
Serves 12.

Michel Richard's French Toast

From famous chef Michel Richard as served at Citronelle, in Washington, D.C.

When I first started traveling around the United States to teach cooking back in the 1970s, Michel Richard's Pastry Shop on Robertson and 3rd Street was the only place where I wanted to eat while in Los Angeles. The food was so good and the desserts so fabulous that I returned there every time I was in the city. I remember begging him to come "East" and to write a cookbook. Fast forward—Citronelle, Michel's East Coast, award-winning restaurant is in Washington, D.C., and he has written two cookbooks.

You will be amazed how easy and quick it is to prepare this pastry custard cream. This silky filling will delight anyone who tastes this French toast. For more of Michel's fabulous recipes, read his magazine *DC CHEFS* or his latest book, *Happy in the Kitchen*.

Custard Cream

1 cup milk
1/4 cup sugar
2 large egg yolks
pinch of salt
1/2 teaspoon vanilla extract
2 tablespoons cornstarch

12 pieces of sliced stale white bread
1/2 cup orange juice
2 large eggs
1/4 cup sugar
1 tablespoon butter
sugar to taste, about 4 & 1/2 teaspoons, plus sugar to mix with raspberries
    (optional)
1 cup raspberries (optional)

Prepare Custard Cream by mixing the milk, sugar, yolks, salt, vanilla, and cornstarch in a glass bowl or microwave bowl.

Place bowl in the microwave for approximately 4 minutes on high.

Remove bowl from the microwave. Mixture should be the texture of soft whipped cream or pudding. Whip the cream with a hand mixer.

Return bowl and mixture to the microwave once again for approximately 2 minutes.

Remove and cover with plastic wrap, pressing wrap directly on top of custard. Set aside to cool.

When custard is cool, lay 6 slices of bread on your workspace.

Whip the cream once again. Spoon about 1 & 1/2 tablespoons of the custard cream into the center of each slice of bread, dividing and utilizing all of the custard cream. Then spread it around with a metal spatula.

Top with another slice of bread, then gently push down on the bread. Set the bread aside.

In a large bowl, whip together the orange juice and eggs, then beat in the sugar.

Soak both sides of the custard cream-filled bread in the orange juice/egg mixture.

Heat a large skillet (preferably Teflon) and melt butter. Lightly sauté the French toast "sandwiches" on both sides until golden brown.

To serve, place French toast on a cookie sheet and preheat oven to broil.

Sprinkle top of each "sandwich" with about 1/4 teaspoon of sugar and place under an oven broiler for a few minutes to caramelize, being careful not to burn the sugar.

If desired, place 1 cup of raspberries and sugar to taste in a blender to make a raspberry sauce. Plate French Toast with Raspberry Sauce.

Serves 6.

Oven-Baked Orange French Toast

I only recently recognized the similarity between this and one of the original "French toasts." This recipe was given to me many years ago when I was first married. Besides making it for "sleep over" guests, I make it for myself as a quick meal (served with some yogurt or fruit) when I don't feel like eating a big dinner.

6 to 8 stale slices thick sliced challah (about 1-inch thick)*
1/4 cup butter
1/2 cup sugar
2 large eggs, beaten well
juice and grated zest of 1 orange
1/2 teaspoon vanilla extract
1/2 cup milk
1/2 teaspoon salt
confectioners' sugar to sprinkle on top

Preheat the oven to 450°F. Place the butter in a 9x13-inch baking dish and melt, being careful not to burn it.

Make sure it covers the bottoms and tilt to butter sides.

In a large bowl, mix together sugar, eggs, zest, vanilla, milk, and salt. Pour into the baking dish.

Place the bread slices in the mixture, allow them to absorb the liquid then turn the slices over. If you don't want to bake this right away, cover and refrigerate overnight, and bring to room temperature before baking.

If baking immediately, bake for 15 minutes, watching carefully so the bread does not burn.

To serve, sprinkle with confectioners' sugar.
Serves 4.

*I trim the "humps" off the top of the challah so I can get more pieces in the pan. I cut others to fit along the long side of the pan and cut others to fit in empty spaces. If you only have pre-sliced challah, then just put one slice on top of another and treat as one thick piece (the recipe will still work fine).

Raspberry Almond French Toast with Frangipane

When Cooks & Company in Indiana, held a contest during their annual brunch class, this was voted the all-time favorite French toast.

4 stale brioches or 16 small slices stale challah, cut into 1/2-inch thick slices
1 cup frangipane (recipe follows)
3/4 cup good quality raspberry preserves
3 large eggs
3 large egg yolks
3/4 cup milk
1/2 teaspoon almond extract
2 tablespoons unsalted butter
confectioners' sugar

Preheat oven to 350°F. If using brioches, slice each in 4 horizontal slices.
Spread half of the slices of brioche or bread with 1 & 1/2 tablespoons of frangipane.
Spread the remaining slices generously with raspberry preserves and put together with frangipane-coated slices, coated sides together, to make 8 sandwiches.
In a shallow baking dish, whisk together the eggs, egg yolks, milk, and almond extract.
Place the sandwiches in the mixture and let them soak about 20 minutes, turning occasionally.
Melt the butter over low heat in a large skillet.
Sauté the sandwiches about 3 minutes per side and transfer to a baking dish.
Bake about 10 minutes to melt the fillings.
Dust with confectioners' sugar and serve immediately.
Makes 4 servings.

Frangipane

1 cup blanched almonds
1 tablespoon all-purpose flour
8 tablespoons unsalted butter, room temperature
1/2 cup sugar
2 large egg yolks
1 & 1/2 teaspoons almond extract
pinch of salt

Combine the almonds and flour in food processor bowl and process until
    finely ground. Transfer to a bowl and reserve.
Process the butter until smooth. Add the sugar, egg yolks, extract, and
    salt. Process until fluffy. Add the ground almonds and combine by
    pulsing.
Refrigerate until firm enough to spread, about 1 hour.
Makes 1 & 1/2 cups.

Strawberry-Filled French Toast

If you have fond memories of cream cheese and jelly sandwiches, you will appreciate this deluxe version of French toast. And if not, perhaps this will entice you to start your own food memories. Any favorite flavor of jam can be used and served with matching fresh fruit if desired.

8-ounce package cream cheese, softened
12 slices of stale bread
1/2 cup strawberry jam
3 large eggs
1/2 cup milk
1/2 teaspoon vanilla
1/4 teaspoon nutmeg
1/4 cup butter

Preheat the oven to broil. Place the oven rack about 5 to 6 inches from the heat.

Spread the cream cheese on six of the bread slices then spread the jam over the cream cheese.

Top with the remaining bread, creating 6 "sandwiches." Cut each "sandwich" in half diagonally to form triangles.

In a pie pan or shallow bowl, beat together the eggs, milk, vanilla, and nutmeg.

Place the butter in a 10x15-inch baking pan and place under the broiler just until the butter melts.

Dip each of the "sandwiches" into the egg/milk mixture, turning to coat all sides.

Place in the baking pan and broil for 2 to 3 minutes on each side or until golden brown.

Serve with fresh strawberries, maple syrup, or dust with confectioners' sugar if desired.

Serves 6.

Variations could include:

Sweet: Cream cheese mixed with jam or fruit preserves; diced dried apricots and slivers of candied ginger; fresh sliced bananas mixed with a little honey; peanut butter and jelly for the kid in all of us; fresh fruit; and grated dark chocolate.

Savory: Add fresh or dried chopped herbs that complement your filling. Suggested fillings could be grated cheese, vegetarian sausage, and smoked salmon and cream cheese with chopped dill.

Delectable Others

*H*owever we use it, bread follows us during each day, from breakfast to bedtime tea and will always be an important part of our lives. In fact, most of us eat nearly twice our own weight in bread each year. There is good reason to call it the "staff of life."

The recipes in this chapter focus on dishes prepared with bread that don't quite fit into any of the other chapters or categories, but deserve to be included. Who could resist a chicken salad made without mayonnaise or a fabulous Passover kugel made from small pieces of matzah (farfel)? These easy to prepare delectable dishes are a boon for any host or hostess.

Apple Charlotte with Apricot Sauce, from the White House

*"The Charlotte brown, within whose crusty sides
A belly soft and pulp apple hides." (1796)*

A "charlotte" is a lovely English dessert, served hot or cold, that is piled high in a lined mold of sponge cake or bread strips. Fruit charlottes are made with sweetened fruits set in a bread lining and are served warm. Apple appears to have been the original flavor and still reigns as the favorite, but they can be prepared using a variety of fruits, including apricots, peaches, pears, and plums.

According to food historians, charlottes were "invented" in England the last part of the eighteenth century; cooked charlottes are related to ancient bread pudding, and uncooked charlottes are related to Elizabethean trifles. The splendid pudding appeared in the English repertoire somewhere between 1761—when George III married Charlotte Sophia of Mecklenburg Sterlitz (the charlotte is said to be named for her)—and 1796.

When White House Chef Henry Haller was doing an apprenticeship in Switzerland, one of the dishes he had to prepare for an important exam was an Apple Charlotte. This recipe won the top score. Later when he was the White House chef, the Nixons liked to offer guests this pretty, award-winning dessert.

16 slices stale white bread, crusts removed
1 cup butter, softened
1 cup seedless golden raisins
1/2 cup dry white wine
2 & 1/2 pounds tart green apples, peeled, cored, and thinly sliced
1 teaspoon cinnamon
zest of 2 lemons
3/4 cup sugar
1/2 cup Apricot Sauce
2 cups sweet whipped cream

Preheat oven to 350°F. Place rack on lowest position in oven.

Cut bread into 2x3-inch strips and brush generously with soft butter.

Line the sides of a one-quart charlotte mold evenly with about one third of the bread strips, overlapping them slightly.

Cut the remaining bread strips diagonally in half to make triangular shapes. Line the bottom of the charlotte mold with most of the bread triangles in a spoke-like pattern. Mix the raisins with the wine and set aside.

Melt the remaining butter in a nonstick sauté pan, add the apples and sauté with cinnamon and grated lemon until tender.

Add the sugar, raisins, and wine, and cook over high heat for 10 minutes, stirring occasionally.

Pour mixture into the bread-lined charlotte mold; cover top evenly with the remaining bread triangles.

Bake charlotte for 50 minutes to 1 hour, until the charlotte is firm and the top crust is lightly browned; if top layer becomes too brown before the charlotte is fully baked, cover with foil.

Let cool for 30 minutes on a wire rack before unmolding onto a deep serving platter. Serve with bowls of warm Apricot Sauce and sweet whipped cream.

Serves 6 to 8.

Apricot Sauce

1 cup dried apricots
1 cup warm water
1 cup hot water
1/4 cup sugar

Soak apricots in warm water for 1 hour. Transfer to a saucepan. Add hot water and sugar and bring to a boil. Cook over medium heat for 20 minutes. Let cool slightly. Puree in blender and serve warm. Makes 1 & 1/2 cups.

Sweet Whipped Cream

1 cup very cold heavy cream or whipping cream
4 teaspoons sugar
2 drops vanilla

In a cold mixing bowl, whip cream with sugar and vanilla until very stiff. Refrigerate until serving time. Makes 2 cups.

Whereas egg whites should be at room temperature to whip successfully, whipping cream should be very well chilled. It even helps to chill the bowl and the beaters.

Chicken Dijon

Since I did not want to include recipes that used bread crumbs as a "breading" or "topping" in this book, I would have had to eliminate this favorite recipe (I have prepared it at least once a week for forty years); so I decided to make an exception and include it! Whether I make it for family or company, it is always well received. It can be eaten hot or cold and freezes beautifully.

3 to 4 chicken breasts, halved, with or without skin and bones
1/4 cup canola oil (approximately)
cayenne pepper
1/2 cup Dijon mustard
1 cup fine unseasoned fresh bread crumbs (made by placing bread in processor or blender)
6 tablespoons butter or pareve margarine, melted

Preheat oven to 350°F. Clean chicken and pat dry.
Place chicken skin side up in an ovenproof baking dish.
Brush chicken breasts lightly with oil and sprinkle a little cayenne pepper on each piece.
Bake for 30 minutes. If using boneless breasts, cook for approximately 15 minutes.
Remove chicken from the oven and turn temperature to broil.
Brush the tops of the chicken with Dijon mustard, back and forth three or four times.
Sprinkle the breadcrumbs over the mustard. Drizzle each piece with melted butter or margarine.
Broil for 3 to 5 minutes or until the coating is golden brown.
Serves 4 to 6.

Chickpeas with Toasted Bread and Hummus

Known in the Arab world as *fatta*, this is a wholesome family meal, not usually served to guests (although they are more popular than most company dishes). The word *fatta* describes the crumbling or breaking of the pita bread into pieces, and the dish probably originated as a method of using up stale bread. All *fatta* dishes have a bed of toasted pita bread soaked in stock or cooking broth, a topping of yogurt and toasted pine nuts, and a variety of fillings including ground meat, chicken, chickpeas, or vegetables. This recipe is an adaptation from the *Middle Eastern Kitchen*, by Ghillie Basan.

1/2 cup chickpeas, soaked for at least 6 hours or overnight (a 15-ounce can of chickpeas, rinsed and drained, can be used instead)
2 to 3 dried bay leaves
1 tablespoon olive oil and a little butter
1 onion, chopped
1/2 teaspoon cumin seeds
1 scant teaspoon ground coriander
juice of 1/2 lemon
3 to 5 garlic cloves, crushed
1/2 to 1 teaspoon salt
2 to 3 large pita breads
2 & 1/4 cups thick, creamy plain yogurt (drain a quart of yogurt in a colander lined with a piece of cheesecloth for about 3 hours at room temperature)
a small handful of pine nuts
salt
freshly ground pepper

Simmer the chickpeas with the bay leaves in plenty of water for at least 1 hour, until they are very tender. Drain them and reserve some of the cooking liquid. Remove any loose skins from the chickpeas and heat the reserved cooking liquid with a little salt.

If using canned chickpeas, rinse, save liquid. Heat the oil and butter in a medium-size skillet and stir in the onion and cumin seeds. Once the onions begin to brown, stir in the coriander and the chickpeas. Toss them about until they are well mixed, then add the lemon juice and season to taste with salt and pepper. Remove from heat and set aside.

Crush the garlic and salt in a mortar and pestle or with the flat side of a large knife until a paste is formed.

In a bowl, beat the yogurt with the garlic and season to taste. Preheat oven to 400°F.

Spread open the pita breads, and pop them in the oven for a few minutes, until they are crisp and brown.

Meanwhile, heat a small heavy-based pan, toss in the pine nuts, and roast them until they look nicely browned and oily. Be careful not to burn them.

Break up the toasted breads with your hands and lay them in a serving dish.

Spoon some of the heated cooking liquid over them, making sure they are well soaked, then spoon the chickpeas on top, followed by the yogurt and a sprinkling of roasted pine nuts. Serve immediately.

Serves 4.

Lamb Fatta with Tomato (Ta'laya) Sauce

Food writer and cooking instructor Amy Riolo gave me this version of *fatta*, which is used for special occasions and is currently very popular in Egypt. It combines clarified butter and a spicy garlic-tomato sauce with lamb, rice, and toasted pita bread for a rich main course. In Medieval times, it was prepared without tomatoes because they had not yet been introduced to the Mediterranean region. Cheese and/or spinach *sambousik* are typical accompaniments to the *fatta* served at holiday meals. Although this dish is not difficult to make, it has quite a few different steps, many of which can be made ahead and frozen. Read the recipe through carefully before making it; having all of the ingredients ready will make preparing this recipe much easier.

Lamb Meat and Stock
(This can be made ahead and frozen for later use.)

2 & 1/2 pounds lamb shoulder meat, cubed
lamb bones for stock
2 medium or large onions, quartered
3 green cardamom pods, crushed
1 cinnamon stick

Tomato Sauce (Ta'laya Sauce)
(This can be made 3 days ahead, covered and refrigerated, or frozen.)

1 tablespoon olive oil
1 whole head of garlic, peeled, cloves minced
1 tablespoon distilled white vinegar
2 & 1/2 cups tomatoes, chopped or crushed (liquid can be used if desired)
handful of freshly chopped parsley or cilantro
1 teaspoon dried ground coriander
salt
freshly ground pepper

Rice

2 teaspoons olive oil
1 cup Egyptian rice or other medium-grain rice, rinsed in a colander
2 cups fresh lamb stock
1 teaspoon salt

Bread

3 day old pita breads, torn in half, spread open the pocket and tear into
    2-inch pieces
1/4 cup olive oil
1 teaspoon dried ground coriander
1 tablespoon fresh cilantro or parsley, chopped

Prepare the Lamb and Stock:
Prepare stock by placing all lamb meat and stock ingredients into a large
    (at least 5-quart) stock pot. Fill 3/4 of pot with cold water and bring
    mixture to a boil, uncovered, over medium heat. Remove scum as it
    comes to the surface with a strainer.
After 20 minutes, lower heat to simmer and cook uncovered for 1 to
    1 & 1/2 hours. Strain meat and set aside. Strain broth and return to
    a very low flame to keep warm until needed.

Prepare the Tomato Sauce:
Warm the olive oil over medium heat in a medium-size saucepan. Add
    garlic and cook, stirring, until it begins to color.
Add vinegar, mix well, and allow to cook together 2 to 3 minutes until it is
    mostly absorbed (this poaches the garlic).
Add tomatoes to the pan, mix well, stir in salt, pepper, and coriander,
    and continue to cook over medium-high heat until mixture begins
    to boil

Stir in parsley or cilantro, reduce heat to medium low, and cover pan.

Allow sauce to simmer, stirring every 15 minutes or so, until mixture becomes very thick.

Sauce is ready when it is reduced to less than half of its original volume (about 30 minutes).

Prepare the Rice:

Heat the oil in a small saucepan. Add rice, salt, and 2 cups of the reserved warm lamb stock, and bring to a boil over medium-high heat.

Stir, reduce heat to low, cover, and simmer for 15 to 20 minutes until rice is done.

To Assemble:

Preheat oven to broil. Place the reserved lamb meat on a jelly-roll pan and season with coriander and drizzle with 2 teaspoons of the oil. Place under the broiler for 1 to 2 minutes, or just until meat is warmed through.

Place torn pita pieces on a large jelly-roll pan and broil just until bread begins to stiffen.

Arrange the torn pita pieces in the bottom of a large, shallow serving bowl.

Brush or spread 2 tablespoons olive oil over the top of the pita. Dribble about 2 tablespoons of the tomato sauce over the top of the buttered pita.

Pour the remaining tomato sauce over the rice and spread into a thin layer over the entire dish. Arrange meat in an attractive pattern on top of sauce and garnish with freshly chopped parsley or cilantro. Serve immediately.

Serves 6.

Variation:

To utilize leftover lamb stock, bring it to a boil, add a handful of vermicelli (or "swallow's tongues"—*lisan al asful* pasta) to the stock. Cook until tender. Add salt, pepper, and chopped parsley to taste. This makes a wonderful light first course to the rich *fatta*.

Mango Quesadillas

This can be used for appetizers or as a main course, just make sure you have enough! You can substitute papaya for mango or use both of them.

jar (7 ounces) roasted red pepper, drained
1 teaspoon canned chipotle chilies in adobo sauce or a dash of hot sauce
4 (9-inch or 10-inch) flour tortillas
4 tablespoons (or more) prepared pesto
1 large mango, peeled and chopped into pieces (papaya may be substituted or used in addition)
2 cups grated Monterey Jack cheese with or without jalapenos
about 2 tablespoons butter or margarine (or more)
2 teaspoons canola oil

Preheat oven to 375°F.

Place the red peppers and the teaspoon of chipotle chilies or a dash of hot sauce in the processor and blend until smooth. Place mixture in a small bowl. This can be done ahead, covered and refrigerated.

Place tortillas on a work surface and brush 1 tablespoon of pesto over half of each tortilla.

Sprinkle 1/4 of the cheese and mangos over the pesto.

Fold the other half of each tortilla over the cheese and mango, gently pressing halves together.

Melt a tablespoon of the butter or margarine and the oil in a large skillet over medium heat.

Cook the quesadillas until golden brown spots appear on each side, adding more butter as needed. Transfer quesadillas to a large baking sheet and brush the tops with the red pepper mixture.

Bake the quesadillas at 375°F until the cheese melts and tortillas are crisp—about 5 to 10 minutes.

Cut each quesadilla into 6 wedges and serve with salsa and sour cream.

Serves 2 to 4.

Parmesan Cheese Sticks

Most people can't quite figure out what these are made with. Great with soups or salads or after-school treats for kids. Freeze nicely, or they will keep in the refrigerator for 2 weeks.

2 cups grated Parmesan cheese
2 cups crushed corn flakes (crushed as fine as possible)
approximately 1 & 1/2 sticks melted butter or margarine
1 loaf thin-sliced white bread, frozen (do not defrost)

Preheat oven to 350°F.
In a pie pan or shallow dish, mix together the cheese and crushed corn
    flakes.
Place the melted butter in another shallow pan or dish.
Remove 2 slices of bread at a time from the freezer and trim off crusts.
Dip bread in melted butter, then in cheese mixture.
Cut each piece of bread into 3 or 4 strips and place on a parchment lined
    baking pan.
Bake 7 to 8 minutes or until golden brown.
Makes about 80 strips.

Passover Pineapple Farfel "Bread Pudding"

This wonderful recipe came from one of my students, who is also a caterer. You will find yourself using it as a side dish all year round since it is so easy to make and freezes beautifully. This recipe is served at the Easter tables of my non-Jewish friends because it goes great with lamb!

canola spray for greasing pan
4 cups farfel (pieces of crumbled matzah)
6 large eggs
1 & 1/2 cups sugar
20-ounce can crushed pineapple w/juice
2 sticks butter or margarine, melted and cooled

Preheat oven to 325°F. Grease a 9x13-inch baking pan.

Place farfel in a large bowl and cover with hot water. Let sit for 30 to 60 seconds then squeeze the farfel dry and "toss" in a colander or sieve to drain well.

Beat the eggs in a small bowl. Add to farfel along with sugar, pineapple, and butter. Mix well. Place in prepared baking pan.

Bake for 45 to 60 minutes or until the top is slightly golden brown.

Serves 8.

Picadillo

This is a Spanish empanada filling (with a variety of tastes and textures) that can be used to fill a hot tortilla or a taco. A tortilla is a bread that can be folded, rolled, cut and torn, stacked, served hot or cold, fried or toasted!

2 pounds ground beef
3 tablespoons olive oil
1 cup finely chopped onions
1 to 2 garlic cloves, chopped fine
3 tomatoes, peeled, seeded, and coarsely chopped
2 cooking apples, peeled, cored, and coarsely chopped
4-ounce can chopped green chilies, drained or 1 or 2 fresh jalapenos,
    seeded and chopped
2/3 cup seedless golden raisins
10 pimento stuffed green olives, cut in half
1/2 teaspoon ground cinnamon
1/8 teaspoon ground cloves
freshly ground pepper
salt
1/2 cup blanched slivered almonds
6 to 12 small tortillas, either flour or corn, warmed

Heat 2 tablespoons olive oil in a heavy skillet over high heat.
Add the ground beef and cook, stirring constantly, breaking up any lumps
    in the meat.
When no sign of pink shows in the meat, add the onions and garlic,
    mix well.
Reduce the heat to medium and cook for another four minutes.
Stir in the tomatoes, apples, chilies, raisins, olives, cinnamon, cloves, salt,
    and pepper.
Simmer, uncovered, over low heat for 15 to 20 minutes, stirring occa-
    sionally.
In a small skillet, heat the remaining tablespoon of olive oil over medium
    heat, tipping the skillet to make sure the bottom of the pan is evenly
    coated.

Add the almonds and cook them 2 minutes or until golden brown. Do not
    burn them.
Drain the almonds well and add to the meat mixture a few minutes be-
    fore serving.
Serve in tortillas or in taco shells.
Serves 6 to 8.

Savory Stuffing

Another of my friend Paula Jacobson's fabulous recipes.

12 cups (1/2-inch cubes) of challah
canola spray
3 tablespoons margarine
1 & 3/4 cup finely chopped celery
1 & 1/2 cups finely chopped onion
2 leeks (use all the white and about an inch or two of the green), finely
    chopped
 2 cloves garlic, finely chopped
 2 tablespoons water
1 & 1/2 tablespoons sugar
1/2 teaspoon salt
1/2 teaspoon fresh ground pepper
1 & 1/2 tablespoons poultry seasoning
1 tablespoon paprika
3 cups chicken or vegetable broth, or less (use only enough to moisten
    well)
 1 large egg

Preheat oven to 325°F.

Spray a large (covered) roasting pan well with cooking spray. (Paula makes
    three times the recipe and bakes it in a 7-quart oval Graniteware
    roasting pan which measures 18 inches long by 12 & 1/4 inches
    wide by 7 & 1/2 inches in diameter).

Place bread cubes on a 15 x 10 x 1-inch jelly-roll pan; bake for 10 minutes
    or until toasted. Remove from oven and set aside. Turn oven to 350°F.

Melt margarine in a large skillet over medium heat.

Add celery, onion, leeks, garlic, and water. Mix well, cover, reduce heat,
    and cook 15 minutes or until very tender, stirring once or twice.

Remove from heat. Stir in sugar, salt, pepper, poultry seasoning, and
    paprika.

In a medium-size bowl, beat the egg, then beat in the broth. In a large
bowl, combine bread cubes, celery mixture, broth, and egg; stir well.
Spoon mixture into prepared pan. Bake, covered for 45 minutes to an
hour. Uncover for the last 10 minutes for a crisp top.

Serves 8.

Stuffed Sweet Mini Peppers

These are a healthy alternative to "poppers." They can be prepped a day in advance and baked at the last minute. Because they can be served at room temperature, cooking instructor Amy Riolo uses these great Stuffed Sweet Mini Peppers as appetizers or buffet items.

12 sweet mini peppers (yellow and orange)
4 tablespoons canola oil, divided
2 (3-inch) pieces stale Italian or French bread with crusts, broken into 1-inch pieces
2 garlic cloves
1/2 cup fresh parsley or cilantro leaves
1 teaspoon capers
1/4 teaspoon kosher salt
1/8 teaspoon freshly ground pepper

Preheat oven to 450°F. Slice tops off of mini peppers and remove seeds.

Mix 2 tablespoons canola oil, bread, garlic, parsley or cilantro, capers, salt, and pepper in food processor to form a thin paste. If mixture is runny, add more bread pieces. If it is too thick, add more canola oil.

Carefully stuff each mini pepper to the top with the filling, without puncturing the pepper.

Coat a small baking or loaf pan with 1 tablespoon canola oil.

Lay peppers in a single layer in the bottom of the pan.

Drizzle with remaining canola oil.

Bake 10 to 15 minutes on each side until peppers are soft and slightly browned.

Serve warm or at room temperature.

Serves 4.

Taramasalata

This Greek cod roe dip/spread is sometimes known as "red caviar sauce" and can be used with vegetables, on good bread, or served with fish or other dishes.

4 to 5 slices store-bought fresh white bread, crusts removed
5 ounces cod roe (*tarama*) (part of a 10-ounce jar)
1 small onion, grated
juice of 1 & 1/2 lemons
freshly ground pepper
2/3 to 3/4 cup olive oil (more if needed)
Garnish: chopped parsley and/or black olives (optional)

In a small bowl, cover the bread with cold water and let sit for a few minutes until water is absorbed. Then carefully squeeze excess moisture.

Place the *tarama,* bread, onion, lemon juice, and pepper into the bowl of a food processor fitted with the steel blade.

Pulse to blend until smooth. Add the olive oil slowly through the feed tube while the machine is on, and blend well. Adjust taste by adding a little more bread or olive oil (additional bread cuts the salty taste and thickens the dip).

Cover and refrigerate until ready to use. It keeps (refrigerated) for about 3 weeks if you cover the top with a film of olive oil.

Serves 6.

Throw Out the Turkey—Keep the Chestnut and Sausage Stuffing!

I need a recipe as a starting point, unlike my friend Ellen Coopersmith (a fabulous cook whom I admire because she never measures anything). So it took her about fifteen years to write down the recipe for this marvelous stuffing for me! Be forewarned—it is rich, lavish, and decadent, and not for the faint-of-heart. This is the recipe exactly as Ellen gave it to me.

1/2 pound margarine
1 cup finely chopped onion
16 ounces ground sausage (she uses half mild and half hot)
6 chicken livers, finely chopped
3/4 cup Madeira (Ellen loves the Barbeito Rainwater Madeira) or more for
    moistening
4 cups Pepperidge Farm Herb Seasoned Stuffing Mix
1 or 2 cans whole chestnuts, pureed (15 ounces each)
Cream substitute or turkey stock as needed to moisten, or more Madeira
    (Ellen uses all Madeira since she likes the richness of the wine flavor)

Heat half the margarine in a large skillet, and sauté the onions until wilted.
Add the sausage meat and cook until lightly browned, using a fork to
    break up the meat.
Drain cooked onions and sausage in a colander or sieve and set aside.
In the same skillet, add the rest of the margarine, heat, then add the finely
    chopped livers.
Sauté until well done. Add the Madeira and boil down the liquid until it is
    almost gone.
Scrape the livers and all the pan drippings into a very large mixing bowl.
    Add the onions and sausage and the stuffing mix.
Puree the chestnuts in the blender or food processor, and add to the mix-
    ing bowl with the stuffing.
Mix well and moisten the stuffing with the cream substitute, stock, or
    more Madeira to taste.

Refrigerate, covered, until ready to stuff the turkey. If there is any extra stuffing that doesn't fit in the turkey, place it in a lightly greased covered casserole, moisten it a little more, and bake it for an hour (at 350°F for an hour).

For an 18- to 20-pound turkey.

Turkish Chicken Salad with Walnuts

There are a number of countries around the world that have a very similar recipe to this chicken salad. This dish is ideal for a buffet. It is best when prepared one day ahead. It is not suitable for freezing. (From *A Taste of Turkish Cuisine*, by Nur Ilkin and Sheilah Kaufman)

3- to 4-pound whole chicken
1 whole onion, peeled
1 bay leaf
1 whole carrot, peeled
4 to 5 peppercorns
1/2 teaspoon salt

Sauce:
3 slices stale bread
1 & 1/2 cups ground walnuts
1 garlic clove, chopped
1 cup chicken stock
1/2 cup milk (additional stock, or non-dairy creamer)
dash Tabasco (optional)

Topping:
(optional)
1 tablespoon canola oil
1 teaspoon paprika

Wash and clean the chicken and make sure no giblets are left inside.
Place the chicken in a large pot, cover with cold water, add the whole peeled onion, bay leaf, carrot, peppercorns, and salt.
Bring to boil, reduce heat to medium and cook for 45 to 60 minutes or until chicken is done. If any scum appears, remove it with a slotted spoon. When done, remove the chicken from the pot and save the cooking liquid.
After the chicken has cooled, remove the skin, bones, and any fat.
Shred the chicken into pieces 1 & 1/2 inches x 1/2 inch.

Arrange the chicken pieces in a shallow serving dish.

Place the stale bread, ground walnuts, chopped garlic, chicken stock, and additional stock (or milk or dairy substitute) in a large bowl. Mix well with a wooden spoon, then place mixture in a blender and puree for 3 minutes. Add sauce to the shredded chicken and mix well.

If desired, place the oil and paprika in a small bowl, mix well, and drizzle it over the chicken making round or oval patterns.

Serves 6 to 8.

Wine, Bread, and Cheese Soufflé

This rustic casserole from author Beth Hensperger is a cross between a traditional soufflé and a quiche. It has a crust of garlic-scented bread slices and a filling made with a dry white wine like a Sauvignon Blanc. Whatever type wine you use will affect the character of the dish. This is one of her signature recipes.

6 tablespoons unsalted butter or margarine, room temperature (or olive oil)
2 to 3 cloves garlic, pressed
8 slices (no more than 3/4-inch thick) stale baguette, cut in half *
1/2 cup dry white wine
1/2 cup milk
3 large eggs
1/4 teaspoon salt
few grinds of freshly ground black pepper
pinch of paprika
1 teaspoon Dijon mustard
splash white Worcestershire sauce
1/2 pound (2 cups) shredded Swiss cheese, such as Jarlsberg or Emmenthaler

Preheat the oven to 325°F.

In a small bowl, cream together the butter and garlic.

Spread (just slather on nice and thick) the bread slices with the garlic butter on one side. Arrange, butter side down, to line the sides and bottom of a 1 & 1/2 quart casserole. It does not matter if there are some uneven spaces between the slices, but place as close together as possible.

In a medium bowl, combine the wine, milk, eggs, salt, pepper, paprika, mustard, and Worcestershire sauce with a whisk; beat until smooth, 1 minute.

Add the cheese and stir to combine. Pour into the lined casserole.

Bake 30 to 35 minutes, or until golden brown and the filling is puffed and set.

Serve immediately. Can be made up to 8 hours ahead, unbaked, covered
with plastic wrap, and refrigerated. Bring to room temperature for
30 minutes before baking.

Serves 4.

* Beth uses a thicker (wider) type baguette. Any amount of bread slices is
fine as long as you cover the bottom and one layer up the sides.

Yia Yia Mary's Skordalia (Garlic Sauce)

This could also be referred to as Garlic Lovers Delight! In an age where everyone is worried about health and cholesterol, this Greek recipe is a healthy spread, usually served with boiled vegetables. It can also be served with fish.

1 to 2 head of garlic (depending on how strong you like it)
6 ounces of walnuts or blanched, whole almonds
2-pound loaf fresh white bread with crusts removed
1 teaspoon salt
3/4 cup extra-virgin olive oil
3/4 cup red wine vinegar (or to taste)

Place the garlic and walnuts in the food processor and chop fine.
Place the bread in a large bowl, moisten/wet it and squeeze all excess water out, but be careful to not get bread so wet that it turns into paste.
Using an electric mixer, add the garlic and walnut mixture to the bread.
Begin to beat them together, adding the salt and slowly adding the oil, about 1/4 cup at a time.
When all the oil has been added, slowly start adding the vinegar, continuing to beat until you have a smooth, creamy consistency.
Store in a tightly closed container in the refrigerator. It keeps well for weeks.
Makes about 4 to 6 cups.

Variation:
After preparing the *Skordalia*, the filling can be used in phyllo triangles and baked at 375°F for about 15 to 20 minutes or until golden brown.

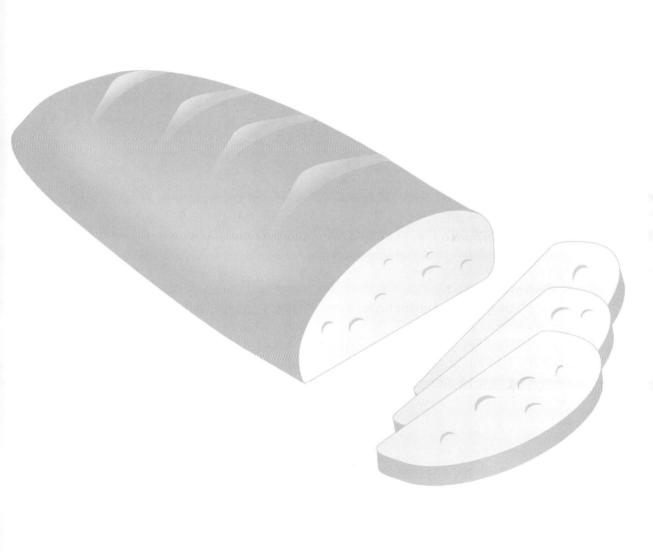

INDEX